The Success Code

The Success Code

How to Stand Out and Get Noticed

JOHN LEES

JOHN
MURRAY
LEARNING

First published in Great Britain in 2016 by Hodder & Stoughton.
An Hachette UK company.
Copyright © John Lees 2016

British Library Cataloguing in Publication Data: a catalogue record for this title is
available from the British Library.
Library of Congress Catalog Card Number: on file
Paperback ISBN 978 1 47362 530 3
eBook ISBN 978 1 47362 531 0

1

The publisher has used its best endeavours to ensure that any website addresses referred to
in this book are correct and active at the time of going to press. However, the publisher and
the author have no responsibility for the websites and can make no guarantee that a site
will remain live or that the content will remain relevant, decent or appropriate.
The publisher has made every effort to mark as such all words which it believes to be
trademarks. The publisher should also like to make it clear that the presence of a word in
the book, whether marked or unmarked, in no way affects its legal status as a trademark.
Every reasonable effort has been made by the publisher to trace the copyright holders
of material in this book. Any errors or omissions should be notified in writing to the
publisher, who will endeavour to rectify the situation for any reprints and future editions.

Typeset by Cenveo® Publisher Services.
Printed and bound in Great Britain by CPI Group (UK) Ltd., Croydon CR0 4YY
John Murray Learning policy is to use papers that are natural, renewable and
recyclable products and made from wood grown in sustainable forests. The logging and
manufacturing processes are expected to conform to the environmental regulations of the
country of origin.
Hodder & Stoughton Ltd
Carmelite House
50 Victoria Embankment
London EC4Y 0DZ
www.hodder.co.uk

Contents

Praise for *The Success Code*

'*The Success Code* is a pragmatic and insightful guide to building reputation and impact that anyone can learn from – even those not in the least bit inclined to self-promote. From communication tips to networking advice, the exercises are sufficiently stretching so there is no hiding behind what 'feels natural'. Written in a manner that helps the reader challenge and reframe some of their anxieties or prejudices about how they approach building their personal brand, the book builds confidence as well as skills.'

Penny de Valk, Managing Director, Penna Talent Practice

'If you believe digital media is for show-offs, not people like you; if you know you should network but don't; if you are told you need to have a personal brand but find the idea distasteful; if you would rather climb the stairs than get in the lift to do an elevator pitch – then buy this book. John Lees is not exhorting you to be different from who you are, he stands alongside you, encouraging you to succeed by being the best authentic version of you. It's a refreshingly different message.'

Dr Carole Pemberton, Executive coach and author,
Coaching to Solutions

'If you dread the thought of 'networking' or 'selling yourself' but want to progress in your existing job and/or future career then this is the book for you. It is full of practical advice and tips and will help you find your voice and achieve success in an authentic way.'

Zoe Shackle, HR Director, AMC Networks International

'*The Success Code* identifies a key issue at work today. Relationships and interpersonal skills are critical to success but not everyone feels naturally comfortable with how they are 'supposed' to behave. John's book helps you to deal with this in a really simple, practical and genuine way with lots of useful insights and tips. It's a great resource in aiding your own development or for someone in your team who is struggling to fulfil their potential.'

Gordon McFarland, HR Director,
Global Professional Services

'Do you want to succeed in your career but cringe at the thought of networking, self–promotion and elevator pitches? This book is for you. The good news: most influence doesn't come from elevator pitches; it's not about conveying information. Influence comes from building relationships. John Lees reminds us that the impression we make matters, and suggests small positive changes that will help other people remember the best of who we are.'

Jonathan Winter, Founder of The Career Innovation Company
and author of The Conversation Gap

'This book is packed with helpful facts, insightful quotes and practical tips. The real appeal for me is the refreshing honesty with which John approaches a topic that many struggle with. He explains that "self-projection" is an important and often misunderstood concept, and we can all improve if we properly plan, prepare and practise. I have never met a successful person who has not benefited from making helpful contacts and yet, from my experience, most people do not understand how to go about forging strong relationships with the right people. Rightly, in my opinion, the book stresses the pitfalls for anyone focused upon self-promotion and, instead, demonstrates that those who show genuine interest in others will ultimately be the people that we wish to approach and keep in touch with.'

Ian Nicholas, Chief HR Officer, REED Specialist
Recruitment Ltd

'*The Success Code* is the book for people who want to promote themselves but are aghast at the idea of coming across like an over-confident salesman in a shiny suit. It's a career dilemma that affects us all: we know we need to put ourselves forward at work, but many of us find the idea of being pushy and networking mortifying. John Lees offers a workable, practical solution. It's self-promotion without the self-regard.'

Rhymer Rigby, freelance journalist and author. His work appears regularly in the Financial Times *and* The Telegraph

'Succinct, well-structured, and very much of the real world, *The Success Code* is founded on good research yet is eminently accessible. This book is for those people who want to progress but don't want to sacrifice their sense of self, who want to amplify who they really are rather than pretending to be something they're not. This isn't a book that berates you and badgers you, it's a book that takes you by the hand and guides you to understanding, and then via understanding into action.'

Kathleen Smith, Business Services Director, the Serocor Group

Foreword

by Sarah Willingham of BBC's Dragons' Den

For anyone who struggles to promote themselves, to progress as quickly as they would like to, to impress the people they want to or to just generally get noticed – this is the book for you!

The prevailing business culture in the UK, and many business advice books, assumes that having an extrovert personality and being an expert in 'power networking' is the only way to get ahead. But this just isn't a natural way of being for 90 per cent of people out there. We can't all become sales gurus and experts in elevator pitches overnight; it's just not in our DNA. The truth is that most of us have personalities that lie somewhere in the middle.

As a TV 'Dragon' and investor, I meet successful and not-so-successful businesspeople every day who pitch me ideas and want to get me to invest in them, and one thing I can tell you is there is no single personality type that automatically gets you ahead in business. I've seen the cleverest people crumble in front of me when faced with giving a presentation, and the most confident communicators present the very worst business ideas.

The Success Code is all about taking control of your own future, about pushing your comfort zone in a controlled way. It's about relationships, looking people in the eye, listening (not just hearing) and returning back to basics where we TALK to people rather than hide behind a screen. The unavoidable fact is that making professional connections is a vital component of a successful working life, and most of the time promotions, job offers and business deals just don't happen unless you're looking your boss, prospective business partner or new client directly in the eye.

In *The Success Code* John Lees has re-written the rules on everything you thought you knew about successful self-projection, networking and effective communication. This book is for you if you dread words like 'networking event' and 'elevator pitch'. Inside, John explains that you don't have to be an extrovert to communicate well. In fact, natural introverts, too often overlooked in business, are very often much better at building relationships as they are naturally better at listening. Whatever your personality type – extrovert, introvert or ambivert – we can all become better at communicating, and more successful in our career progression and business dealings.

In *The Success Code*, John will challenge you to face your fears about self-projection and encourage you to explore what's holding you back from making new connections in your professional life. He'll move to the edge of your comfort zone, and give you powerful tools to control and manage the messages you're giving out, whatever your natural personality type.

What's more, this book is easy to understand, simple to follow with easy-to-use tips, and straight-talking. It will give you the confidence to start networking authentically, and the strategies to start meaningful and productive business conversations naturally. By the end of this book, you'll start to understand how others perceive you, what they say about you when you leave the room, and how you can use this to your advantage. Finally, the strategies inside *The Success Code* will help you move towards getting genuine, warm recommendations from colleagues, clients and business partners, helping you grow your business to the next level and realizing your career goals.

Sarah Willingham
Serial entrepreneur, consumer champion, business-woman, BBC Dragon and mum of four

About the Author

John Lees is one of the UK's best-known career strategists, writing and speaking about the world of work.

He specializes in helping people make difficult decisions about work. This usually involves helping them to reach out to other people, talk about themselves, and make new things happen.

John is the author of a wide range of business titles. His books have been translated into Arabic, Polish and Spanish. *How To Get a Job You Love* regularly tops the list as the bestselling career change handbook by a British author and, along with *Job Interviews: Top Answers to Tough Questions*, has been selected as WHSmith's 'Business Book of the Month'.

Other titles include *Secrets of Resilient People* and *Knockout CV*. He is a regular blog contributor to *Harvard Business Review* online and in 2012 wrote the introduction to the *HBR Guide to Getting the Right Job*.

He appears frequently in the national press and his work has been profiled in *Management Today, Psychologies, Coaching at Work* and *The Sunday Times*. John has contributed to the BBC interactive *Back to Work* series programme, BBC2's *Working Lunch*, Channel 4's *Dispatches* and ITV's *Tonight – How To Get A Job*. John has presented at conferences and events in Australia, New Zealand, South Africa, Switzerland and the United States.

John is a graduate of the universities of Cambridge, London and Liverpool, and has spent most of his career focusing on the world of work. He has consulted for a wide range of organizations including: British Gas Commercial, the British

Council, CIPD, Harrods, Hiscox, House of Commons, Imperial College London, the Association of MBAs, Lloyds Banking Group, Marks & Spencer, Napp Pharmaceuticals, Oakridge, as well as business schools across the UK. John is a Fellow of the CIPD, an Honorary Fellow of the Institute of Recruitment Professionals, a Career Management Fellow, and was a founding board director of the Career Development Institute.

Alongside his day job, John serves as an ordained Anglican priest. He is married to the poet and children's writer Jan Dean. They live in East Devon.

w: www. johnleescareers.com
tw: @JohnLeesCareers

johnlees
associates

Acknowledgements

I am indebted to the work of several writers who have forgotten more about personal impact than I will ever learn. In particular I would point to *The Charisma Myth* by Olivia Fox Cabane (Penguin, 2013), *Influence: The Psychology of Persuasion* by Robert B. Cialdini (Harper Business, 2007), *Gravitas* by Caroline Goyder (Vermilion, 2014), *How to Talk to Anyone* by Leil Lowndes (Harper, 2014), *The Introverted Presenter* by Richard Tierney (Apress, 2015) and *Networking for People Who Hate Networking* by Devora Zack (Berrett-Koehler, 2010).

My enormous thanks to everyone who has helped to shape this book or steer it on its way, including Gill Best, Richard Nelson Bolles (jobhuntersbible.com), Nancy Collamer (mylifestylecareer.com), Hilary Dawson, Richard Doggett, Zena Everett (zenaeverett.com), Peter Fennah (careersynergy.com), Patricia Keener (keenerinspiration.com), Darryl Howes (ddnsconsulting.com), Kate Howlett, Ian Nicholas, Jonathan Poston, Stuart Robertson (sr-associates.com), Richard Tierney (introvertedpresenter.com) and Ruth Winden (careersenhanced.com).

Particular gratitude goes to my wife Jan Dean for untangling several chapters and to Carole Pemberton (carolepemberton.co.uk) for not only contributing ideas but also assuring me that the book was heading where I hoped to point it.

Thanks, as ever, go to my agent James Wills at Watson, Little for his unstinting support and to my Hodder & Stoughton editor Iain Campbell for commissioning the idea and massaging it into shape.

Dedication

This book is dedicated to my great friend Richard Weston.

Richard is not only a gifted professional photographer (find him at Weston Digital Imaging), but an inspiring teacher and mentor – and just about as authentic as they come.

How to get the most from this book

This book decodes success for people who hate the idea of selling themselves.

This is a book about getting noticed, but it's not a conventional book. It doesn't tell you to sell yourself, get out there, impress with power dressing or have an elevator speech.

The pages ahead are a practical guide to making an impression, authentically. It's probably true that about 10 per cent of people will never feel comfortable talking about their strengths, while another 10 per cent need no encouragement at all. This book is for the remaining 80 per cent. People like you who want to make an impression in the world, but don't quite know how to make it happen.

This book will help you if you:

- Hope to build the confidence to approach new people.
- Want to be noticed in a busy marketplace.
- Need to reach out to people to advance your career.
- Need to shape a more positive reputation so that you become a more credible promotion candidate.
- Want to widen your range of connections but you're not a natural networker.
- Struggle to communicate your strengths without feeling like a fake.
- Want work to find you rather than having to constantly chase it down.

You've probably heard of personal branding and you're probably tired of hearing about it. It's too closely associated with self-promotion – pushing to gain influence, exploiting connections and talking too much. But getting noticed doesn't have to mean overselling. Throughout the course of this book, you will discover exciting research, positive psychology and advice from a range of experts that will help you to make an authentic impact.

> By stepping just to the edge of your comfort zone, you will learn to project yourself onto the world of work.

From discussing personal influencing skills to presentations, this book decodes the elements of success for people who hate the idea of selling themselves. You'll rethink networking, learn how to talk about yourself in ways that others find easy to listen to, and also directly influence what people say about you. You'll discover how to project yourself in writing without looking as if you're pushing too hard, and learn how to engage people in a way that sparks curiosity and leads to interesting offers.

The Success Code

I

The power of self-projection

This chapter helps you to:

- Understand that loud self-promotion is not the only way to get noticed
- See the difference between selling and communicating
- Understand why it's often hard to talk about yourself
- Explore why introverts and extroverts operate very differently
- See that self-projection is not just for extroverts, but a vital part of getting results

What is self-projection?

This question may be running through your mind right now, especially if you're the kind of reader this book was written for. This guide serves as an antidote to the bookshelves of material out there that teach you how to be a smooth networker and a great self-publicist. Perhaps you're the type that finds any chance to talk about yourself like pushing against an open door – a welcome chance to 'wow', to make people smile and feel engaged? More likely, you find it hard work; for some it's a nightmare.

Imposing your personality on others is a trend that permeates modern society. Psychologist Tomas Chamorro-Premuzic writes in *Confidence: Overcoming Low Self-Esteem, Insecurity, and Self-Doubt* about a long-term survey of US college students.

In the 1950s, 12 per cent described themselves as 'an important person'; by the 1980s no less than 80 per cent made the same claim. Other studies point to the rise of digital narcissism, including extensive disclosure of personal information and the ever-present 'selfie'. In 2010 researchers at Western Illinois University looked at students who use Facebook, identifying such traits as 'self-absorption, vanity, superiority, and exhibitionistic tendencies' and a 'willingness to manipulate and take advantage of others'.

This book is about **self-projection**. That isn't the same as self-promotion, which is about wanting to impose yourself on other people. To be clear about the behaviours we are discussing:

1 **Self-promotion** is the action of promoting or publicizing yourself or your activities, explicitly, often with some force.
2 **Self-assertion** in its most negative sense is about asserting your superiority; in its most positive sense it is about vocalizing your rights, claims and opinions.
3 **Narcissism**, according to the *Oxford English Dictionary*, is 'a grandiose view of one's own talents and a craving for admiration'. This self-regarding behaviour is often about attracting empty praise and avoiding objective feedback.
4 Other kinds of egotistical **self-centred behaviours** are easy to spot – believing that the world is all about you and it's not worth listening to anyone else, or putting your own interests first.
5 **Self-projection is something very different**.

You will find the word 'projection' used differently elsewhere. Psychologists talk about projection as an unconscious transfer of desires or impulses to another person, as in 'it's your fault I had to shout at you'. In this book I am using 'self-projection' in a slightly unconventional but very literal way – like an image projected onto a screen. The screen is the community of people you want to share information with. What you project is what you decide to show on that screen.

Think of the different ways in which you project yourself. This might be in great detail (for example, in a CV), or whatever pops out of your mouth at a party when someone says 'now tell me about yourself...' (*see* Chapter 3 for the pros and cons of the Elevator Pitch). It could be in everyday conversation. How much of what you say is remembered? What will others say about you when you're not around? My working definition of self-projection is: *how you help others understand and remember important things about you.*

Why self-promotion doesn't have to be the norm

Pushing yourself forward in a 'me-first' style seems widespread and has acquired an air of social acceptability. In her book *Quiet: The Power of Introverts in a World That Can't Stop Talking* Susan Cain reports that during the 1920s people were invited to believe that success and better health could be obtained simply by acquiring charm and avoiding an inferiority complex. Cain argues that society has a 'cultural bias towards extroverts' and 'nowadays we tend to think that becoming more extroverted not only makes us more successful but also makes us better people'. She shows how in US colleges, outgoing, assertive behaviours are reinforced through praise; students feel they will receive lower marks if they do not impose their personalities in a group setting.

This creates huge tensions for individuals from cultures that see such behaviour as crass or rude. Studies by psychologist Robert McCrae show that personality types are not distributed evenly across the world – a much lower rate of extroversion is found in East Asia compared to Western countries. Japanese and

Chinese students attending Western business schools can find that their quieter manner is misunderstood in team discussions. Their comparatively gentle approach arises from a concern not to embarrass or outshine other people; an uninformed observer might see it as a lack of enthusiasm or assertiveness.

Cain outlines the value that introverts bring to a range of contexts and roles, arguing that thoughtfulness is a helpful and undervalued component of business decision-making. Many writers today share her notion of the **ambivert** – someone in the middle ground between extrovert and introvert. Some psychologists argue that a large part of the population occupies this space, and recent writing offers a range of strategies to help quiet and mid-zone people rethink the way they interact with the world – and to find an operating style that both feels true to who they are and gets them the results they're looking for.

Party animals vs. wallflowers

Some people are naturally comfortable with self-projecting; others need to work at it. Where you sit on the extrovert/ introvert scale depends on the starter kit you've been given from the gene pool. Extroverts generally love company, introverts less so. Introverts prefer to think then speak after they have processed what they are going to say; extroverts often say 'I don't know what I am thinking until I have explained it to someone else'.

Rather than risk inadequate definitions, I'm turning to a trusted friend who understands psychometric testing better than anyone I know. Business psychologist Stuart Robertson is author of the Quintax personality questionnaire (sr-associates.com).

Introversion and extroversion

In my personal view, introversion–extroversion is a broad domain in personality which includes a number of components influencing how we act and interact with people and situations. Each component has a 'polarity' with roughly opposite behaviours at each end. For example, being relatively friendly and relaxed about approaching people (extrovert pole) has its opposite in being more independent, and less energized by social contact, even a little aloof (introvert pole). Extroverts are more interested in making and maintaining social contacts; introverts prefer self-reliance.

We might think about where people derive energy – extroverts do so from the outer world of action and social connection, introverts from the inner world of reflection and ideas. When it comes to risk-taking and adventurousness, extroverts often have a 'do-think-do' cycle where introverts may adopt a more cautious 'think-do-think' cycle. Extroverts tend towards spontaneity, liveliness and even an impulsive approach to decisions while introverts take a more prudent, thoughtful approach.

Different levels of comfort with self-disclosure are also evident. Extroverts are often more open with others about their feelings, introverts more private and selective about who they share with, and how much information they feel comfortable imparting and receiving.

We may show broadly introverted or extroverted styles – or a balance between the two, sometimes in apparently contradictory ways. For example, an adventurous person may turn out to be relatively self-reliant and less sociable. Or an outgoing person seems risk-averse in action, perhaps shy in less familiar social settings. Other examples include the serious academic who inspires admiration through unexpected humour, and the shy actor.

While they permeate our whole approach to people and things, extroversion and introversion rarely exist in pure or consistent forms. They are not simply about whether one likes social contact. They help condition what we feel is the most appropriate and desirable way to behave, moment by moment in the world.

In a climate where introversion is sometimes seen as a form of weakness, you need to remember that both extroversion and introversion have their strengths. It's also important to note that shyness and introversion are not the same thing.

'Shyness is the fear of social disapproval or humiliation, while introversion is a preference for environments that are not overstimulating. Shyness is inherently painful; introversion is not.'

Susan Cain

I'm happy to talk about any subject except myself

Some people are relatively good in social situations, but hate talking about themselves. What makes people react so differently to the same context? Shyness, self-esteem, and confidence are important factors. You may find it easier to talk about a product, service or idea than talk about yourself. Actors often say they can speak the words of a playwright with great confidence, but some find it hard to appear in public 'out of role', as themselves. So this difficulty appears to be partly about the role you occupy, and partly about subject matter — the things you have to talk about.

Legitimate solutions come from two angles. One is about thinking, the other about behaving (*see* 'thinking and behaving' in Chapter 2). Thinking differently can be about standing back from yourself and acquiring objectivity. It can be about reframing (for example, operating as if you're doing things on someone else's behalf). It can also be about taking the focus away from yourself and your anxieties. These are some of the strategies you'll discover in this book.

Behavioural change is also powerful; don't underestimate the power of experimentation. You can get better at self-projection even if you're relatively shy – repeated exposure to situations where you need to talk about yourself makes the process feel easier and more natural.

How 'selling yourself' gets in the way

As you will read in the pages ahead, one thing that goes wrong for people trying to make an impact is starting with the idea that they should be selling themselves. As Chapter 3 explains, it's the dominant message in most advice about networking and personal branding. And it's completely wrong.

Most people dislike being on the receiving end of a sales process. You immediately associate it with cold selling – the telephone interruption when you're at home relaxing, or the fundraiser who blocks your path with a cheery but determined expression. When buying something you're more open to a salesperson who finds out about your needs rather than one who tells you what you want – building curiosity rather than pushing a sale. Average sales training is about communication; excellent sales training is about asking questions.

If you feel you're being sold to, you sense that you're the second most important person in a conversation. You feel under unwelcome pressure. It's okay to be sold to when you've given your permission and you can choose the setting. For example, nobody likes being sold to in a social context. Research in 2012 from ExactTarget showed that only 4 per cent of social media users in the US would look at Facebook to find a promotional deal, even from companies that have been given permission to send them offers. It stands to reason that you're going to be more resistant to being pitched at when you're enjoying yourself – so meeting someone at a party who insists on explaining the benefits of his services is a big turn-off.

'Overtly selling yourself is just embarrassing for you and embarrassing for the person listening to you. People put up all kinds of barriers if they feel they're being sold to. Many professionals are developing a completely different approach to selling – sometimes described as a feminine approach – more listening, less broadcasting. I encourage people to learn to talk about what they've done with confidence but also with dignity.'

Kate Howlett, transition coach

Self-projection is about having proper conversations, not holding an audience captive. The word 'conversation' is defined by the *OED* as 'a talk, especially an informal one, between two or more people, in which news and ideas are *exchanged*' (my emphasis – note that it's a two-way flow). The Middle English roots of the word convey a familiarity and intimacy, and the Latin *conversari* means 'keep company (with)'. Conversation is not primarily about information or influence, but about getting on with each other and sharing experiences.

Ruth Winden agrees that to 'sell yourself' is the wrong starting point:

'Instead, think of those people who provide a genuine service that fulfils real needs. Or think nurses, doctors, IT consultants, or restaurant owners. Even if you don't work in sales, who do you serve? What needs do you fulfil? In what way? And if you want to serve even more people, or provide an even better service, then surely you'd do yourself and others a disservice if you weren't prepared to talk about it? Can you see how sharing what you do and achieve, from a positive intention, can be a genuine form of self-projection?'

Ruth Winden, social media expert & career coach

What the 'sell yourself' school forgets is that in effective conversations, both parties communicate and listen – a conversation feels more meaningful if you can make a valid contribution to it. Where your 'conversation' is an overt and uninvited sales pitch, you could be trashing the chance of a genuine relationship for the pleasure of hearing yourself speak.

Shaping what people say about you

Shaping what people *say* about you starts with influencing what people *know* about you. If you exert no influence and take no responsibility for how people describe you, you get results that are, at best, random – and, at worst, undermining. If people hear only negative information about you (which could be as simple as the suggestion that you're lacking direction), that's not a matter of chance. You've let that news get out there. It comes from something you said, or something you failed to say. If your LinkedIn page gives out a vague or misleading message, that's what people notice, not your experience.

This issue will be dealt with extensively in the chapters ahead, particularly Chapter 4. For now, let's agree some ground rules and share some good news.

The ground rules: if you want to make changes in the world, even small ones, you sometimes need to influence people as well as inform them. There are many ways to do this, all pointing towards one outcome: people will be saying the right things about you.

And the good news? The very good news is that you have far more influence over what people say and think about you than you imagine. It's not a matter of chance or dependent on the whims of others. You are in charge of the message, and you decide what's in it.

By the time you've worked your way through this book something different will be happening. You'll have taken the first steps in cracking the Success Code. If your name comes up in your absence, you will know why, and you'll have a pretty good idea about what will be said. Because you will have written the script.

Crossing the gulf

Newcomers to the art of self-projection often report a gulf between what they want to communicate and what they actually say. Sometimes the words that come out of your mouth sound wrong. You hear the advice 'just be yourself' but find it unhelpful. After all, you present several different 'selves' at work to match particular circumstances. You behave differently talking to the boss compared to work colleagues. You'll act very differently in a formal presentation than passing on information over lunch.

Better advice would be to 'be the best version of yourself that you can bring out under pressure'. This starts with visualizing, then practising how you behave in the spotlight. You don't need to transform yourself overnight. You don't need to be a fake. But you can learn to present the most upbeat, enthusiastic and energized version of yourself. This starts with remembering what you are like when you are at your best, on a great day when things are going well. Start by remembering what that person is like. Remember a brilliant day at work. How did you see yourself on that day? You can use this technique to reconnect with positive energy and your 'best self'. This is reinforced by rehearsing good stories where you convey some of the energy of the original event.

Why self-projection matters

We self-project because we're genetically programmed to do so. Plants use colour to reproduce (ripe fruit reddens to show it's at the prime stage to be consumed). Animals use body colour, posture, body language and sound to warn, impress or attract. Humans project, too, sometimes in colour or physical gesture, but also in words. We have subtler, more complex messages that we want 'on screen', out there, remembered.

So, uncomfortable as it can be sometimes, you need to project messages about who you are, which means you'll need to get used to the idea of talking about yourself. Decoding success means getting to grips with self-projection in a style that works, authentically, for you. You will have to present ideas, impress, become known as the go-to person. There will be many times when you will need to outline your contribution at the drop of a hat, not just when you're seeking a promotion. Outside work you'll be asked 'and what do you do?' – sometimes having a memorable answer to this innocuous question can make a big difference to the next stage of your life.

Think about what you communicate without thinking. Be honest – what's the immediate impression you make when you arrive at a meeting or stand up in front of even the smallest audience? Do you appear competent, focused, on message? Do you seem in control? Do you look and sound like someone ready for advancement? Work on how you imprint on other people's attention; you'll be surprised how often 'maybe' turns to 'yes' in a wide range of work conversations.

Don't stay locked in reflection. Use the ideas presented in these pages to change what you *do*. You might think that the chemistry between you and others is entirely instinctive and outside your control. That's just keeping your head in the sand. Small adjustments to the way you come across can make a huge difference. Thinking about the pros and cons of talking about yourself means that the focus is on you. Imagining the possibility of future relationships puts your focus on other people.

Reputations are shaped, held and communicated by relationships. There are some things in life you can do unassisted but most require at least one conversation. Entrepreneur and former ice hockey player Rich Stromback sees a balance between the need for selective connection-making and the need to become known:

'I need to be selective, yet authentic; focused, yet open to possibilities. Opportunities do not float like clouds in the sky. They are attached to people.'

What is the Success Code, and will you know you've cracked it?

The Success Code is hidden to many people. They haven't understood the power of authentic influencing. They believe there's only one way of making progress in life. Decoding success means that you learn to think differently.

This book helps you decode behaviours that some people use instinctively, and others take time to learn. Mastering the Success Code takes two steps. You understand that you have the ability to influence how others think about you. Secondly, you influence in a style that works for you. You'll be taking yourself just outside your comfort zone, but the journey will provide exciting results.

Top 10 messages from this chapter

1 Self-promotion can be narcissism wearing a business suit. Self-projection is about authentically communicating.

2 Assertive and outgoing may be the social norm, but thoughtful people who listen make a big contribution.

3 Introverts tend to avoid self-disclosure and high-energy communication, but this restriction is strongly influenced by context – and preparation.

4 People enjoy being listened to and having their interest sparked. They don't like the pressure of a sales pitch.

5 Don't allow yourself to believe that talking about yourself is the same as self-promotion. It isn't.

6 Telling and 'pitching' are less effective than building curiosity.

7 It's important to decide in advance what you want to communicate – the specific messages you want people to remember.

8 The first step is to find a dignified but also effective way of talking about yourself.

9 The advice 'just be yourself' is unhelpful. Dig deeper to remember what you were like when in a positive mode.

10 Taking the first step is often about taking the focus off your anxieties and imagining the benefits of new relationships.

2

The way you communicate shapes your world

This chapter helps you to:

- Understand the power of communication to change the way people see you
- Remember how much more goes into communication than words
- Explore how work communication differs from other contexts
- See how reputations are shaped, developed, degraded
- Understand how others influence the way you are seen

Everyone broadcasts

You communicate all the time, transferring information. Sometimes communication is purely about data transmission: 'My train gets in at 11.02' or 'I need that enlarged to A3'. Often it's more complex.

Whether you are aware of it or not, you're in 'broadcast' mode all the time. Active or relaxed, your facial muscles present a picture. When you've switched off you may look intelligent, sleepy, friendly, irritable. Some people look stern and unapproachable when they are at rest. Airline cabin crew and others in customer-facing roles learn to exert control over these facial expressions so that they project warmth and openness. Controlling the face you present to the world is helpful in other contexts, for example at a conference when you want to show that you're open to speaking to new people. Some people do this instinctively, some try too hard and end up projecting discomfort rather than a genuine smile. You can learn how to project a version of yourself that looks and sounds natural even though you've worked on it.

The way you communicate shapes the way you are seen by others. This is the big theme of this book, but let's take a simple example to start. Consider the impact when you call in for your morning paper – what impression do you leave? Are you always complaining: about traffic, the weather, litter? If so, you'll probably be remembered as the customer who grumbles. If you always sound cheerful and often say something nice about the way the shop is looking, you'll be remembered and talked about very differently.

Language is amplified by tone, body language, style, emotional state and context. Saying 'can I make you a coffee?' to your life partner is social noise that is hardly noticed. Being the first person to offer a drink to a client who has just arrived at your workplace, who is feeling somewhat ignored, can make the difference between a successful deal and lost business.

Moving towards more effective communication

You have two severely underestimated capabilities:

1 You can **learn to observe** how you communicate and are understood.
2 You can **learn to change** how you communicate and are understood.

Here 'understood' contains more than you might think – when people understand what you're looking for and what you offer, they can move you in a new direction.

One of the mistakes average communicators make is believing that everything is instinctive or it's all about personality – you've either got it or you haven't. That radically underestimates the power of insight, preparation and rehearsal. The important thing is to decide what you are trying to achieve – and to focus your actions on this goal. Is your plan to make someone feel they're interesting and worth your attention? If so, you can begin to adjust your behaviours. Intention and action must be linked, otherwise you'll become one of the many who say they want to build relationships and then act as if the opposite were true (*see* Chapter 6 on persuading people to help you without getting in their faces). Intention is critical to sustaining changed behaviours.

Context and purpose

The manner in which you say things is strongly related to context: you speak differently in a meeting to the way you speak to your colleague at the next desk, and differently when addressing someone very senior. Even outside work it's easy to slip subconsciously into different communication modes. For example, if you want to impress you may subtly suppress a regional accent, speak more slowly than normal, and use longer words than you would usually. Context is everything. You may be saying something about what you want or need, or explicitly trying to influence the future. So context is linked to *purpose*.

Some conversations are purely about enjoying other people's company. Chatting with a family member you'll probably say pretty much anything you like, switching topics suddenly, speaking in 'insider' language – including family code and jokes – and you can be moderately unpleasant, cynical, disgusted, disappointed, wildly optimistic or joyful without any real long-term impact on relationships. Here interactions are largely social – even though there are goals in mind, getting on with people is what matters.

Other conversations are completely transactional. In a DIY store you might approach a salesperson with a friendly smile but you aim to quickly mention the product you're trying to find or the problem you're trying to fix. Most, but not all, people ring call centres wanting to state their problem immediately and eliminate the small talk.

Many work conversations fall into another category. By 'work' I mean any context relating to employment, self-employment, getting and keeping jobs, finding customers, making an impact as a professional, even some aspects of your studies. Work frequently blurs the edges between the transactional and social. Sometimes discussions are about informing, telling, instructing, but far more often they're about consulting, persuading, testing the temperature. Work-based communication always has a purpose in mind. Conversations are often about influencing, monitoring, managing, implementing change. Having tea with friends is about enjoying each other's company; tea taken with a former boss probably indicates an agenda.

The word 'agenda' shouldn't sound sinister. Conversations can have agendas – when both parties can see there are specific and predictable outcomes in mind. These might be outcomes which help both parties (e.g. a consultation or a customer service call). At other times the needs of one party take priority (e.g. a briefing meeting or listening to a set of instructions). With an agenda in mind, there is pressure, sometimes mild, sometimes strong, to reach an acceptable outcome. Conversation style changes – communication becomes more structured, information is exchanged more deliberately and agreements and actions voiced.

Agendas mean that you start to think, often instinctively, not just about outcomes but about structure. When you say to a friend 'there's something important I need to explain to you', that's social code for 'I'm asking your consent to dominate the next few minutes with a single topic of conversation'. It may even be code for 'don't distract me with your concerns, and don't interrupt too much' – even casual agenda-setting is very clear about tone, mutual roles and rules of engagement.

With an honest understanding that there's *always* an agenda, it now becomes important to really think about communication. It's not just about speaking, but doing several other things at the same time.

Being clearer about your agenda

Do you need the *facts* to be clear? If so, think of a way of making them relevant to the listener. If you say things that don't make a connection, what you say may remain part of the everyday overflow of information.

Are you communicating too much? You may disclose only part of the information you have at your fingertips.

How consciously are you communicating *intention*? When you listen to other people you'll often be asking yourself 'what does this person really want?' or 'what am I being asked to do, and how do I feel about that?' or...

How transparent are you being about what you are saying? You may be explicit or guarded about outcomes – each strategy gives you a different kind of result.

How far are you communicating in your role? Roles can be explicit, assumed or unclear – for example, you may not always find it easy to tell the difference between an order and a suggestion from a manager.

How far are you, unconsciously, communicating a state of being? It's easy to signal your mood, confidence levels, working style, attitude to others around you, or your ability to read a context. Getting this right – indicating that you are an easy person to have a conversation with – is a powerful communication tool. Getting it wrong may mean you're undermining what you're trying to achieve.

Influence outweighs information

Sometimes we pretend that information is the only thing being exchanged. Consider the way people talk about how old they are. They can disclose their age with embarrassment, disarming honesty or pride. Reflect on how you say an ordinary word like 'no'. Even in a text message this word can cause huge offence, even though it may be a simple statement of fact. A simple question like 'are you free for lunch?' can be affectionate, caring, concerned, subservient, seductive, attention-seeking, dominating, needy, resentful – and can probably carry a thousand other nuances.

Information is a small element of communication, and often the least important part. In some contexts it's almost irrelevant. If you're in a war zone or reconciling factions in a community, for example, sometimes all that matters is that people are talking with each other, not what gets done.

As we develop as working humans, attuned to the nuances of the workplace, we learn that interactions during employment are not just about saying things in the way we want, but saying things in the way others need to hear. Inexperienced people blame others for not listening properly; more mature workers understand that even in everyday interactions you need to think about your audience and impact.

When conversation tips into speech-making

Sometimes nothing at all gets through.

'The single biggest problem in communication is the illusion that it has taken place.'

Irish playwright George Bernard Shaw

'The two words "information" and "communication" are often used interchangeably, but they signify quite different things. Information is giving out; communication is getting through.'

US journalist Sydney J. Harris

Poor communication happens for many reasons. Sometimes you're unclear about what should be said; at other times you don't find a way of saying something so that the recipient really hears it. Speech-making does this – producing long, pre-prepared statements or stories with little regard for the actual conversation. You'll find people who do this at networking events – for more *see* Chapter 9.

What you communicate just by being there

Humans have built-in mechanisms giving us early indications if we're in danger or in safe company, and we pick these signs up mostly from body language and facial expressions. Stanford University psychologist Nalini Ambady studied the way we make early judgements about whether we are in tune with people. Ambady prepared very short video segments of lecturers at work. University students who did not know the lecturers were asked to score these teachers on a range of personality characteristics. Ambady showed that videos as short as six seconds were sufficient to form an impression of character every bit as accurate as evaluations from students who had been in real lectures. We make very rapid decisions about whether we find people confident, competent and easy to talk to, largely based on a snapshot impression.

Someone you approach at an event is therefore processing a lot of information fast – deciding whether talking to you will be an enjoyable experience. As soon as they begin talking to you other decisions start to form – am I curious about this person's experience? The impact you make isn't just about the opening moments of a conversation. Curiosity opens the door to a deeper level of connection, which means that there is now a reason to keep in touch. What's more, something of what you have said will be remembered.

Leakage – the things we don't intend to communicate

In conversation, even if you're talking about relatively neutral subjects, you'll convey something of your mood. If you tell a story it's usually evident if someone has pleased or irritated you. If you find a topic dull this is often clear from the way you talk. Better communicators know how to suppress these signals.

However, that's fine when you're calm and prepared. When the heat is on, your natural operating style reveals itself. You might say you're a consultative manager and good at sharing information, for example. However with a deadline looming or in crisis you may unconsciously behave in the opposite man-ner – *telling* rather than *asking*, and making decisions without checking how they impact on others.

Tired, unwell, under pressure or distracted, self-awareness can easily switch itself off. That phrase 'under pressure or distracted' can however describe the most ordinary kinds of distraction. Magicians and pickpockets know how easy it is to distract attention, to trick the brain into missing something important. Under emotional pressure you might struggle with simple tasks like remembering your banking PIN or a colleague's name. You can very easily drop your guard and leak emotional informa-tion. Remember a time when you had to do something routine after an event that you found shocking, such as a road traffic accident? For a period of time everything you said and heard was coloured by that experience.

We 'leak' clues about our emotional state frequently, often without realizing it. Remember a moment in the past when you experienced a disappointment – perhaps you presented an idea to a meeting and it was shot down in flames. Your funding application was turned down. You failed to win an award. Some people take routine knockbacks like this in their stride with no impact at all on their work performance; most people experience at least a short period of self-doubt, which can easily communicate itself when you're talking about something entirely different. This means that it's often wise to avoid communicating difficult things when you're less attuned to how others are reacting.

You broadcast on several wavelengths simultaneously: words, how you say them and the body language that either reinforces or undermines those words; it's easy to say one thing and communicate another through non-verbal channels. Sometimes the words you use are like an ill-fitting suit. For example, the graduate attending her first job interview may have been told to start sentences with: 'I am skilled at…'. However, if this lacks conviction and sounds coached rather than true, it can easily come across as 'I'm saying this but don't really believe it' and 'I have potential but little real experience'. A confident candidate may get away with a sentence that begins 'I am skilled at…', but it rarely sounds believable the first time out. When you make claims it helps if they are grounded in hard evidence. This is why stories are often much more than assertions – 'I did' is usually more convincing than 'I am'. Confidence and feeling authentic are strongly linked. A better prepared individual might say 'let me tell you about the last job I did…' or 'let me tell you how I handled that', focusing on the story rather than the storyteller.

Small steps to better conversations

When Dale Carnegie published his massive bestseller *How to Win Friends and Influence People* in 1936 he didn't plan to preach to the converted. He wanted to change the mindset of all kinds of people.

He wrote the famous line: 'You can make more friends in two months by becoming interested in other people than you can in two years by trying to get other people interested in you.'

He also wrote: 'It isn't what you have or who you are or where you are or what you are doing that makes you happy or unhappy. It is what you think about it.'

You can't change behaviours just by thinking, but the process of *deciding to act differently* is one of the most powerful in human experience – in other words, intention. If your intention is to shape your future, even to a small extent, by influencing others (in an open, non-manipulative way), you've taken the first step towards what others will see as visibly changed behaviours.

Let's take a great example outlined by the writer Leil Lowndes. In *How to Talk to Anyone* she points out the number of famous people who offer a sustained, personable smile. When you greet new people you tend to smile as a social courtesy, but it's often a very quick facial expression that can easily look cursory.

Lowndes' 'Flooding Smile' works like this:

'Don't flash an immediate smile when you greet someone, as though anyone who walked into your line of sight would be the beneficiary. Instead, look at the other person's face for a second. Pause. Soak in their persona. Then let a big, warm, responsive smile flood over your face and overflow into your eyes. It will engulf the recipient like a warm wave. The split-second delay convinces people your flooding smile is genuine and only for them.'

Thinking and behaving

You may assume that some aspects of personality are pretty much fixed from birth. However, the way you project that personality outwards is far more under your control than you would like to admit. It's easy to hide behind the statement 'this is the way I am'.

The architect and designer Richard Buckminster Fuller once wrote:

'If you want to change how someone thinks, give up. You cannot change the way people think. Instead, give people tools that help them do something different.'

The Franciscan writer Richard Rohr reframes another well-known idea:

'We do not think ourselves into new ways of living, we live ourselves into new ways of thinking.'

To change your outlook, you need to adopt new behaviours. Your brain wants to reject this idea by pretending that the sentence above reads 'you have to learn to think completely differently and change everything about your behaviour'. That's a great recipe for avoiding even the smallest change. Over-processing (*see* Chapter 6) can seriously get in the way, but so can black-and-white thinking. Watch out too for mental stop signs like 'I can't', which usually means 'I haven't tried enough angles yet'.

Watch out too for absolute statements like 'I'll never be comfortable talking about myself'. What happens if you learn to be just a little bit more comfortable? Beware 'this isn't going to work for me'. What if you get just 10 per cent working for you? Then 10 per cent more? The Zone System in Chapter 10 takes you from the inner recesses of your comfort zone towards conversations with a range of interesting people. The Appendix offers some Starter Scripts in support.

One bit of thinking that might be getting in your way is around shyness or nervousness in social situations. You don't want to be around new people, and feel inhibited when it happens.

'Up to 13 per cent of people will suffer from social anxiety disorder at some point in their lives. Social anxiety comes from a fear that you might say or do something embarrassing and others might think badly of you. Without treatment, social anxiety can be persistent and disabling – it stops people from doing things they want to do – like meeting new people, building relationships, chatting to colleagues at work, going to university, going for a job interview or going to the pub with friends.'

Oxford Centre for Anxiety Disorders and Trauma

Overpreparation can get in the way as well. This can mean learning long pitches that no one can interrupt. If you believe that you have to make at least half a dozen strong points when you speak it means that your attention is directed internally. You're listening to *your* 'script', not to the person who wants to be the matching half of your conversation. You're observing yourself rather than paying attention to someone else. That's why some people come across as distant, as though they're not fully present in the room. Give yourself a break by learning to listen, allowing the conversation to draw you along rather than always wanting to steer it (*see* Chapter 6 on better listening).

Top 10 messages from this chapter

1 You broadcast all the time, consciously and unconsciously.
2 Communication is about a great deal more than information.
3 Don't believe that your personality dictates everything about the way you behave.
4 You can learn to see yourself better and improve the way you communicate.

5 You don't need to change all your behaviours over-night, but start somewhere.

6 Be clear about *why* you are communicating before you think about how.

7 Watch in particular how you communicate under pressure or when you are tired.

8 The most important and difficult kinds of communication are when you are trying to influence something outside your direct control.

9 You shouldn't shy away from the idea of having an agenda behind what you communicate – it helps you to be clear about purpose.

10 An initial impact matters, because that's where the first and possibly last decision about you is made.

3
A new take on personal branding

This chapter helps you to:

- Rethink the concept of personal branding
- See the dangers of trying to become a brand that doesn't fit who you are
- Avoid judging yourself in comparison to others
- Begin to reach out to people and know what to say about yourself
- Learn to grow rather than trying to fake it

Can a person be a brand?

Branding – an overview

Decoding, noticing and communicating brand information is what consumers do every day. As your eye tracks along supermarket shelves your brain seeks out products you know and trust. Brands are about memory and emotion; marketing budgets ensure that when brands come to mind we remember favourable characteristics, such as reliability, quality, value for money. We feel safe around brands, they enable us to make easy purchasing decisions, and we recommend them to people who matter to us.

'Although we think that decision-making about brands depends strongly on functional benefits, it all comes down to one question: how will this make me feel?'

Kim Cramer and Alexander Koene of
Amsterdam branding consultancy BR-ND

The reason we select, recommend and stay loyal to brands is that they connect with our emotions. Brand identification is part of the way we make sense of the world. Brands work. Get branding right and your product dominates the public's imagination.

Does 'personal' branding make sense?

So, if brand impact is what persuades buyers to repeatedly commit, surely that's a concept we should apply to human beings? After all, we want to be picked for tasks, remembered when promotions or awards are on offer, be identified as a supplier, fixer or information broker. How do you make an impact and stay at the forefront of people's minds? How do you regularly and consistently receive recommendations as *the* 'go-to' person?

Personal branding seems to hold the answers to these questions. Many self-help books and motivational speakers argue that people are brands just as much as products or organizations are. A brand is identifiable, frequently remembered and associated with favourable qualities – and so, the argument goes, are people.

We can certainly learn something from the emotional impact of strong brands. Some marketing experts argue that 'brand love' is a myth or a thing of the past. Advertising budgets tell a different story: large organizations want you to buy their stuff and feel their products are like trusted friends. Branding seeks emotional triggers including excitement, surprise, wonder, confidence, safety and nostalgia, and we can see some of these elements in the soundbites you use to recommend someone as, for example, 'a safe pair of hands' or 'full of ideas', or someone who 'gets the job done'.

Are people more than simply brands?

You might argue that human beings are more complex and less consistent than products. We change and develop. Products are generally predictable in their performance, while people have off days. With products brand love is a one-way process; you may love your favourite shampoo, but it doesn't love you back. Where the brand is a service or an organization there is often a real relationship. You may have a very strong brand loyalty to the person who cuts your hair or your favourite plumber. The fact that brands are sometimes bound into real relationships can also be a weakness, of course. When your favourite coffee shop has a change of staff your loyalties may change overnight (and it's often said that a service brand is often only as strong as the last point of contact). How you feel about an electricity provider will often be strongly influenced by the last conversation you had with one individual in a call centre.

So, brands sometimes involve people and rely on them, but does that really mean that you as an individual are a brand in your own right?

One of the problems surrounding this idea is where it comes from. Personal branding is championed by some of the highest-performing communicators known to humankind – motivational speakers. They seem to know everything about how to get 'out there', making an impact in any situation from one-to-one pitches to presentations to large audiences. These individuals appear to perform with great impact and energy (what you may not see is how withdrawn they can be offstage). The message they act out seems to be: 'become like me and your life will be changed'. This of course plays to audience insecurity and envy. Many of us secretly yearn to be somebody else, if only for a day. How often do you imagine your problems would be solved if you could be exactly like your role model? The idealized other person here could be a work colleague, a fellow student, a sibling or a TV personality – any source will do.

Personal branding is an idea, a fashionable one, pitched to us just like any other idea in our culture through a heady mixture of argument, persuasion and emotional manipulation. Surely you want to be more impactful, interesting, attractive? Surely you want more confidence? These are the leading questions used to persuade us to buy something, and motivational speakers know the techniques well.

Think about the kind of people who are telling you how to be. Compared with 50 years ago you rarely hear voices in the media that encourage you to be more reflective, to look at issues in depth over time rather than rushing to judgement. Instead, you have a wide range of up-front, direct, confident personalities – because these are the activist voices and behaviours loved by the media. How many people do you see on TV who give their opinion only when they have thought carefully about a question, or only speak when they have something to say? TV's primary filter puts style before substance – even university professors only get their own series if they have a colourful presenting style.

Some branding ideas help when you want to shape your reputation

Some people have little interest in the way they affect others, and achieve results ranging from brilliant to embarrassing. Self-awareness is something that enables you to modify behaviours and grow, but (as Chapter 6 shows) can also get in the way. Even if you don't buy into every aspect of personal branding, seeing yourself as others see you is a key stage in self-development.

As with brands, a number of important questions come to mind:

What are you known for?

- What's the first piece of information that comes up when your name is mentioned?
- How positive is that piece of information? How clear is it?
- Does it help you or get in the way of progress?
- Is this information a fair and accurate summary of what you can do?
- Are you associated with one area of expertise or many?
- If you're known for more than one thing, does the overall mix make sense?
- What kinds of projects or tasks would you like to be recommended for?
- What handful of ideas or facts would you like people to remember the next time they hear your name?

Think about people who haven't thought about these questions.

Take Derek as an example. He finds his job boring and wants to move on. He tells his friends about his boredom, but says nothing about what he'd like to do next. His LinkedIn page is sparse and two years out of date. People know he's unhappy, but have no idea how to help him change this.

Take Jane as another example. She set up a professional photography business 12 months ago. She has a big social circle and often talks about her work. She often says unflattering things about her customers: 'everyone with a camera thinks they can take wedding photographs' and 'customers think they can do better with a smart phone'. Her friends sympathize, but if asked to recommend a photographer for a family portrait, they don't suggest her. They want to recommend someone who takes great photographs but also makes the experience enjoyable.

Contradictory messages or overlapping expertise?

One of the reasons why some people abandon the idea of communicating their 'brand' is that they value their own complexity: 'I don't want to be labelled' and 'I don't want to be known for just one thing' are commonly said. In the checklist 'What are you known for?' above question 5 is about being known for more than one thing. We dislike labelling (*see* 'positive pigeon-holing' in Chapter 11), and yet apologize where we present two or three different areas of expertise. Ironically, this can be what makes you distinctive, possibly unique.

When one person recommends another, they often describe a cluster of qualities and information rather than making just one statement or using one phrase to describe you. So don't hide behind the idea of 'I'm complicated' or 'what I do doesn't make sense' – it's your job to shape your material into a memorable bundle of ideas, clear enough for others to pass on: 'Lucy's a great designer; her HR background means she's fantastic with people, and I love the way she brings ideas from her history degree into her work...'

The dangerous game of comparisons

In a situation where you have to influence someone (for example at an interview or in a meeting with your boss) be aware of false comparisons. You start with a picture of how you think you will act. This could be a fairly positive picture, or tinged with doubt. If there's some performance anxiety, this picture may have negative shading. For example, you might be making a sales pitch, very aware that the last time you did this you felt you made a mess of things. You might be asking for a promotion, remembering that on a previous occasion you received a flat 'no'. It's easy to colour the picture with darker tones and predict failure as the likely outcome.

Before long you're feeling that everyone manages these situations perfectly well – and you're the only one with difficulties. You've talked yourself into believing that your working style contrasts with the 'norm'. This 'norm' is, of course, a false construct – your ideas of how 'everyone else' does things. You've created two false and contrasting pictures more coloured by emotions than facts. One picture shows you at a low point, the other is an idealized picture of how others perform. As the antique maps used to say, *here be dragons*. It's all too easy to believe that everyone performs better than you.

So, another picture comes to mind – how someone else would behave in the same situation. As we discussed above, it's easy to believe that you need to be a perfect copy of someone else. Constantly feeling 'I will never do it as well as X' is very limiting – you need to develop behaviours that work for you, not mimic others. However, you can observe and learn. 'Borrow' behaviours – particularly from people who are like you but have more experience. For example, watch people who present quietly, modestly but still effectively. People who can win others over without over-selling. People who can say something about their own skills and know-how without bragging or dominating.

Your picture of what you are capable of achieving begins with your picture of others, particularly those you have ranked as star performers. Look at the people you have adopted as role models. Do you learn from them, or just put them up as a perfect standard you'll never reach? Think about anyone who regularly gives you advice – particularly if their communication style is more extrovert than yours. Will the model they present work for you? A well-trained coach will draw out the best version of you, but other influencers may essentially be saying 'become *me*'. These may well be the people telling you to 'get out there... work the room' and – you knew it was coming – 'you need an elevator pitch'.

Is an elevator pitch vital?

The elevator pitch (or speech) is a way of summarizing your strengths in a short, high-impact statement. The phrase seems to have developed in the last century as smart advice on being succinct and punchy when you've got somebody's attention. The scenario is that your boss gets into the lift and, just as she presses the button for her floor, asks you to talk about what you do for the business. Your answer, it's suggested, should be short enough for a brief elevator ride, but also memorable and positive. Proponents argue that we should all have a 'pitch' (anything from 60 seconds to three minutes is recommended) ready for any similar context – for example at an event when someone says 'what do you do?'.

'A good pitch should answer three questions: Who are you? What do you do? What are you looking for?'

US writer Nancy Collamer

The most helpful aspect about the idea of the elevator pitch is understanding that an embarrassed silence and over-delivery are to be avoided: it's certainly better than staring at your shoes, being tongue tied or rambling on endlessly without really saying anything. It's a good reminder that there are times when a practised script can rescue a tricky situation; using a script so it sounds genuine is a different matter. Some people try pitching once or twice and, not enjoying the results, drop the idea. Others avoid the activity entirely, describing the process as 'slick' or 'cheesy', resembling the way politicians speak on TV.

The problems of pre-constructed speech are legion. An elevator speech can easily feel like someone else is speaking. The words are those you don't recognize. Just as some people can carry off a bad joke while others provoke an embarrassed silence using exactly the same words, a 'pitch' can add to your difficulties rather than solve them. It may just feel wrong, particularly if it's scripted in the kind of language you don't normally use.

Often, people say too much. When people try to influence in writing (*see* Chapter 11) they sometimes put down every fact and argument they can think of in the hope that something will hit the target. Similarly, in an elevator pitch people try to get multiple strong points across. One elevator pitch model recommends that you say something about where you grew up, where you live now, current family situation, current role and what you do for fun, and also include something about your personal characteristics, recent roles, how you plan to provide immediate value to the organization and, finally, your values and what motivates you. To get that all into 60 seconds means you're going to have to gabble like an auctioneer.

'Too much' is often linked to 'too soon'. We're encouraged to pitch early, to get the message across while you've got someone's attention. This can also end a conversation very swiftly. You don't want to talk this way, and other people don't want to hear it.

The problem is the word 'pitch', suggesting that you're only interested in someone if they become a customer. It's the first step towards believing that the only point in human conversation is to sell something. Studies that focus on what prompts customer responsiveness show that it relies on the experience of being listened to, and feeling that information is being shared. Overt pitching is a blunt instrument. You can find a thousand websites telling you that communication is all about selling; fewer tell you why people dislike being *sold to* (*see* Chapter 1).

'Elevator speeches are such an outdated concept. Who wants to be talked at, pitched at and sold to these days? People are a lot more sophisticated and discerning in what they pay attention to, so we need to adjust communication if we want a positive response. This all starts with listening more, understanding what the other person is interested in and finding out how one can be of help. Introverts are at a distinct advantage here – they naturally create space for communication as they tend to listen carefully and take time to respond, rather than barging in and pushing their own agenda.'

Ruth Winden, social media expert & career coach

Producing a better overview

There will come a point when you not only get a chance to talk about yourself, but it's appropriate to do so. Putting aside the razzmatazz of the Elevator Pitch, what can you say that won't make you or your listener cringe? How can you convey information that someone will find interesting, relevant and will propel the conversation in a useful direction? Learn how to deliver summary statements, keeping things brief and to the point.

Top 10 tips for shaping effective Summary Statements

1 Don't start with a written script. You don't speak the way you write. Start by speaking out loud. Record what you say, then write down useful phrases.
2 Use the phrasing you would normally use in everyday speech.

3 Practise a statement out loud at least three times. When it flows, rehearse with a friend.

4 Keep it short. Focus on saying less, but in the right way, rather than saying more and doing it badly.

5 On the other hand, avoid cheesy one-liners. Saying 'I connect people and ideas' may sound enigmatic, but it's slightly pompous and doesn't help someone understand you any better.

6 Try beginning with a question or example: 'You know all those photographs you have on your laptop and you can never find the specific one you are looking for? I show people how to find any image in less than ten seconds.'

7 Use a statement when it feels right and you really need it.

8 Have alternative ways of getting information across, such as chatting naturally about what you do.

9 Aim for warmth rather than dynamism. Talk with people, not at them.

10 Don't forget that the main reason why someone will want to connect with you isn't because of the content of what you say, it will be because they feel a connection with you personally.

For great advice about improved summary statements look at the wealth of tips on the Internet helping scientists explain their roles in understandable terms. Nancy Baron, Director of Science Outreach at COMPASS in California, suggests you use four headings: 'the problem, why it matters, potential solutions and the benefits of fixing it'. One of the techniques suggested is to begin your explanation with an illuminating question, such as: 'Did you know that half of the antibiotics prescribed by GPs in the UK have no impact on a patient's condition?'.

Why you don't have to fake it

Classic fixes designed to help people 'get out there' are all about transforming you into someone else – the confident, articulate performer you believe will always be one step ahead of you in work. This idea wastes a huge amount of energy and talent. You don't need to transform yourself into someone else, or pretend. You don't need to hope that you will, against all odds, suddenly become the most confident person in the room.

'Faking it' a little on a physical level can help. Professor Amy Cuddy of Harvard Business School asked subjects to adopt both high-power and low-power physical poses, measuring both psychological and physiological effects. The study found that positive body posture 'changes body chemistry' – faking high-power poses caused people to become more confident and willing to take risks, while low-power poses cause people to feel helpless.

You can adopt strategies that enable you to communicate confidence and energy, but trying to talk yourself into being someone else is crazy. What works is this: *learn how to be the way you are on a good day*. Replicating the behaviours you bring out, unconsciously, when things are going well, when you're appreciated, when you have something to say. That's not how you are every day, but you have behaved that way before, and not by accident. Don't pretend that those confident behaviours were nothing to do with you. Somewhere *you* have been clear, confident and interesting. The problem is drawing that performance out under pressure. Start by remembering and then drawing energy from your past into the present (*see* Chapter 12 on running the right kind of movie).

Rather than planning to transform yourself completely, go for small improvements. Do it one sentence at a time. Rehearse better opening statements for when you meet people. Practise a short, natural answer to the question 'what do you do?' – something calm and clear rather than a clumsy elevator pitch. Work on smarter questions to get people talking. Move up just one gear and things start to change. But don't be happy with just one level of improvement. Keep practising, keep changing, keep adding more of your best self to your ordinary self.

Top 10 messages from this chapter

1 Don't allow yourself to be browbeaten by the idea of personal branding.
2 Think about what you want people to remember about you and say about you.
3 Don't judge yourself in comparison with extrovert networkers and communicators.
4 Don't be bullied into an elevator pitch. If it feels wrong it will come out wrong, particularly if you lack practice.
5 Start thinking about more comfortable ways of talking about yourself and your abilities without them sounding like ego statements.
6 Remember that influence comes from relationships, not just information. Seek conversations, not opportunities to talk about yourself.
7 Look hard at any technique that makes you feel inauthentic.
8 Build on confident moments from your past. Recapture how you felt at your most relaxed and confident, and let that underpin your actions.
9 Don't feel you have to fake it or pretend to be somebody else.
10 Take small steps to improve your performance rather than looking for overnight transformation.

4

What people say about you when you're not in the room

This chapter helps you to:

- Understand how information about people is remembered and passed on
- See how reputations are shaped, developed, degraded
- See how fear of rejection limits what you ask for
- Gain insights into the way key messages about you travel unassisted
- Progress from getting mentioned to being recommended

How information about you arrives

Although close friends and family know a huge amount about you, most people don't. They don't need to – yet. This chapter explains two important ideas about how you influence others and how your reputation is shaped. You project yourself onto the world through what others say about you. You have far more control over this than you imagine.

How might someone else discover you? We stumble across people all the time, both online and in person, when we're looking for something in particular and when we're not actively looking at all. If someone comes across you, how will they decide they want to speak to you? They could look you up online. Somebody might pass on your CV or business brochure. An email originally from you might be forwarded.

However, the most likely method won't involve written text at all.

The most likely route is that your name will feature in a conversation. Think about that moment. In the same breath as your name comes up so will some information. This could be 'make-or-break' material – words that recommend. What specific words will they be?

When I'm working with clients who want to get noticed, I enjoy asking my first question: *What do people say about you at work when your name comes up?* This sometimes draws a complete blank, but a client's first guess is usually around personality: 'they would say I'm a positive team member' or 'I'm easy to work with'. It's possible that something might be said about your character, but this will probably be as an add-on. You wouldn't stop a colleague in the corridor and say 'I've just met a really nice guy!'. You might, however, hold the lift to say 'I've just met someone you really need to speak to'.

How much information?

When you begin the process of self-projection you'll find yourself saying too much, too little or the wrong things. It's as inevitable as first mistakes made in dating. Too much and you sound both confused and desperate. If you've ever listened to someone give a 'summary' of their experience that takes ten minutes you know about over-supply. Many people do this in writing as well, sending a two-page letter when a two-line email will do.

Your CV probably contains well over a hundred pieces of data, your LinkedIn page about the same. Some of this is neutral, some of it even negative, some important. The problem is that if you swamp someone with information, they don't know which parts to process or use. They don't know which specifics to remember, so they just remember feeling confused.

Look at this from another perspective. How much information do you pass on when you recommend someone?

The power of three

Here's my second coaching question on this theme: Imagine two people meet at a coffee machine at work tomorrow. Your name comes up in conversation. How many pieces of information about you will be mentioned in the time it takes to dispense just one cup of coffee?

Most people think about how little time is available, and say 'about three things'. In fact, 'about three' tallies with everything we know about communicating and retaining information. When a public speaker wants to make an important point, it's normally composed of three elements and repeated three times. When a politician is interviewed on the morning news they will usually focus on getting two or three clear messages across. If someone says 'let me tell you three things I like about this brand' you'll listen carefully for items one, two and three. The busy human brain likes short sequences because they're easy to absorb and remember.

However, the power of three can also work against you. If you've upset someone recently or done a bad job, all three items could be negative.

Alternatively, you could have planted negative messages yourself. Imagine one of the individuals at the coffee machine had lunch with you just the day before, and you talked at length about the way things were going badly for you. Now the three items passed on might be 'Jane's feeling a bit low. She didn't win that big contract. In fact, she's thinking about moving out of consultancy work'. The three slots available to you have been used up with information that might win you sympathy but probably won't make your phone ring.

Controlling the message

The issue here, as Chapter 1 outlined, is control. If you're not in control of what you communicate, your results will be unpredictable. If you broadcast random information, you will get random results. If your LinkedIn page leaves people confused or with an unhelpful picture, that's because you have decided to present it that way. The way people 'read' you and what you offer is not a matter of chance. You've put that picture out there.

As we've discussed, one amazing result of unlocking the Success Code is you discover that you have far more power than you've imagined. You can directly influence what people say and think about you – not by selling yourself or over-asserting, but by being disciplined about giving people only a small handful of news items you hope they will remember – two or three positive points they will find useful and interesting.

You're in charge of the message, and you must decide what it says. By the time you've worked through this book something different will be happening. If your name is spoken in your absence, you will know why. And you'll have a pretty good idea about what items of information will come up – because you will have written the script.

When chat becomes recommendation

The manner in which someone voices your name varies considerably. A **mention** means you're simply named, perhaps as one of several useful people. You're in the race, but you're not the favourite thusfar. You haven't yet reached the world of recommendations, but you're in the territory called **referral**. This may be **active** (deliberately passing on a name to someone who will find it helpful) or **passive** (when faced with an issue or problem you remember someone useful). As discussed above, you get a referral if there are positive reasons to do so – plus an obvious match between problem and solution (*see* Connection Statements in Chapter 14).

A referral is helpful, but it doesn't become a **recommendation** until it includes warmth and certainty. A referral says 'you could think about giving the work to Alice'. A recommendation says: 'Alice is the person you need, no question – she's great to work with'. That phrase paints a picture of a future working relationship that is enjoyable as well as productive. It also projects certainty. A recommendation says 'you're safe here'.

A warm, no-holds-barred recommendation like this takes some beating, but think about what goes into it: sound knowledge of Alice's abilities and why she should be recommended, plus an implied reassurance of performance. A strong recommendation is pretty close to a **guarantee**, which is why you don't make them every day. When you do, you put your reputation on the line. If the person you recommend lets someone down, that damages *your own* credibility. That's why you need to plan to build relationships – so that people not only understand what you do well, but feel so confident about your track record they will invite others to trust you.

Working out your messages

This book talks about messages. People get confused by this word – think of a message as 'a controlled packet of information'. For example, you might want people to know that you have worked in an unusual mix of sectors, or you trained with a particular expert, or you know your way around a software application. These are clear and distinct messages. Information is more likely to travel if the message is short and distinctive.

That doesn't mean it has to be unique. Don't get hung up on the idea that you should have a Unique Selling Proposition (or USP). That tough and unlikely standard can seem so out of reach that you may end up saying nothing about yourself because you feel you should be talking about unique characteristics or experience. It's much more common that, after doing some thinking, you can describe a distinctive mix. That might be a very simple combination of facts: 'I trained as a musician but I work in graphic design now'. It might be that you have an unusual combinations of strengths – you can do both people and technology, for example.

Holding out for one unique selling point sets the bar far too high. You're better off looking for interesting things to say about your story. This may take you far less time than you think. Think big picture rather than detail. You might list all the details you would put in an online profile and then try to pick out your strongest points. That has the merits of collecting good evidence (great for when you need to give examples of what you have done), but can be laborious. Try the exercise below.

Exercise: grabbing the headlines

Print out your CV (or your LinkedIn profile). Place it face down on a table so you can't read it. Get a friend to ask you the following questions, and to write down your answers. Try to answer concisely, but don't worry if the right words don't come straight away.

Question 1: 'What do you hope people will say when they recommend you?'

Your first answer needs to get past the need for personal reassurance ('I hope they say I am a person of

---

integrity/fun to work with/reliable') and move towards work – 'I hope they say I'm brilliant at analysing information'.

Question 2: 'What are you known for?'

Brief your friend to probe for details. So if you say 'I'm a good people manager', you need the questioner to say 'What kind of people? How do you manage them?'

Question 3: 'What do people say about your skills?'

Again, your friend needs to probe and check. Make sure you are talking about skills (things you do) rather than personal qualities. Your questioner should keep asking the question 'What else?' until you run out of ideas.

Question 4: 'What do people say about your experience?'

Remember this isn't a list, but an overview. What sectors have you worked in that might make you stand out? What organizations have employed you?

Question 5: 'What do people say about your areas of knowledge and expertise?'

More probing and checking. This works really well with someone who isn't familiar with your field of work so they need to ask questions to understand what you're trying to get across.

Question 6: 'What makes you a bit different?'

Think hard about what you have already said. What combinations of skills, experience and knowledge are likely to get you recommended?

By this point your friend should have written nearly a full page of bullet points. Now turn your CV over and you'll see why you've kept it face down all this time. How many of the important points you've just made appear in your CV? Key points will be missing. Adding your new bullet points is your starting point. You also need to edit this material down until the list is the right length: small enough to communicate effectively but long enough to get your key messages across.

Why do you need someone else to help you with the Grabbing the Headlines exercise? Simply because you need to talk and think while someone else writes things down. Find someone good at asking 'What else?' and then allowing silence – good questions ensure you are clear, specific and move away from generalizations. It's also a good way of starting to talk about yourself, developing a style that is easy to understand, interesting and relevant to the someone else's perspective – if your friend doesn't get the message, what chance do you have of impressing a stranger?

Working towards recommendations

If you have got the right messages working on your behalf, you will get a recommendation. The strength of that referral depends on the impulse behind it. The referral could be 'you could do worse than talk to Jane' going right up the scale to 'Use Jane. I can't think of anyone better'.

How does this happen? Here are some possibilities:

- Your name comes up in conversation because someone has talked to you recently.
- Someone enjoyed meeting you and wants to talk about the experience.
- An email or letter from you has sparked someone's interest.
- Someone has seen a piece of work you've produced and is talking about it.
- A question has been asked and your name comes up as a potential answer.

- Someone identifies a problem or need and you come to mind as a potential solution.
- Someone has described what the ideal consultant/supplier/candidate/contact would look like, and you are identified as a potential match.
- Someone has been impressed by you and wants others to know that.
- Someone is organizing an event or a meeting and they want you to be there.

This list isn't exhaustive, but captures some of the most important turning points. Any one of the above could lead to an offer, an invitation, secondment to an exciting project, a funding offer or a promotion. This isn't – largely – about luck, because most of these outcomes happen because you did something to start off a chain reaction.

If you think about each of the contexts outlined above, one thing they have in common is *trust*. You mention people for all kinds of reasons – frustration, irritation or just to tell a good story. However you recommend people, or talk positively about encounters with them, it's because of trust. That doesn't mean people need to know you very well. This isn't the deep trust that comes from long-term friendships. The unspoken message behind a positive recommendation is 'I trust this person, so you can too'. In that moment, when someone says 'give Jane a call', the person recommending you trusts you to fulfil your part of the bargain.

When someone recommends you they trust you to do things like this:

- To respond warmly or at least politely if you are approached.
- To recognize the name of the person recommending you.
- To listen carefully to requests for proposals or information.

- To deliver on time and be a quality provider.
- To honestly say if you can't help and offer other solutions.

Isn't that a huge amount to expect? Yes, certainly. That's what a warm recommendation is all about. This isn't somebody saying 'Jim will be no worse than anyone else'. This isn't someone saying 'Eve will take your call if she's not too busy'. A recommendation contains a huge amount of unwritten information, and arrives in an envelope of trust. We recommend brands because we believe they will add something to other people's lives – and people for the same reason.

Outcomes and fear

Starting to manage what people will say about you means focusing on **outcomes**. Outcomes here can be subtler than Dale Carnegie's 'win friends and influence people'. Think about the outcomes that are important to *you*. For example, you might want someone to remember you as a skilled project manager. You might want someone to know you've won an industry award. You might want someone to know you're fascinated by health monitoring technology. *How* you get this across matters far less than the fact that your message sticks.

Don't set your goals so high you'll never take a step towards them. What steps could you take to achieve such a tangible referral? You might post out copies of an article you've written, or email a list of projects you've managed. You might choose to go to an event focused on your area of expertise, or pick up the phone to someone who has engaged you in the past. The 'how' is open to negotiation and exploration. The end result is the thing to keep in mind, and try to take regular and consistent steps towards achieving it, bearing in mind that your best results will nearly always come from face-to-face conversations.

We're often vague about intentions — not because of lack of imagination but because of fear. For example, if your aim is to get a specific person to recommend you, you're probably already thinking 'what if she says no?' and 'what if he doesn't feel my work is good enough?' Because you're afraid of hitting the 'no' brick wall, you pretend you're open and leaving things to chance: 'I'll talk to Doug and see what happens...' Planning your messages makes the difference between random and focused.

This fear of rejection also makes you hear a 'no' when the word hasn't been spoken. Let's say you ask a former boss for a recommendation. He says he'd be happy to consider this but wants to know a lot more detail about your next role. He wants to tailor the reference, but what *you* hear is hesitation, perhaps even reluctance, and you don't ask your boss for help again.

Take another example. You're at a conference and want to have a conversation with the last speaker. You stand in line and can see that the speaker is busy. When you get there, instead of beginning a conversation, you give a reason for avoiding one: 'I expect you're too busy now...'. This implies that the speaker won't make time for questions, and also that you're easy to get rid of. Fear has reshaped your intention of 'I really want to speak to this expert' into 'I'm going to give permission for an instant brush-off'.

Anticipating worries about rejection can lead to very different outcomes. So, approaching your conference speaker, put your attention on how you want the conversation to end, not its beginning. Don't apologize for taking up someone's time, don't give a long introduction about yourself, and don't ask a rambling, complex question. Use gentle determination: 'I enjoyed your talk very much. The question it prompts for me is...' If the speaker seems eager to leave, have a good back-up line: 'I wonder if we could have a conversation later when things are quieter for you?' If the speaker is swamped with questioners, ask for a phone conversation later in the week, but be clear about boundaries and expectations: 'I'd like to ask you just a couple of questions. Perhaps I could ring you later this week? Don't worry, I promise not to take up more than ten minutes of your time'.

Top 10 messages from this chapter

1 Information about you – positive, negative and neutral – travels, whether you want it to or not.
2 Intention is critical. What do you hope to achieve when you communicate? If you don't care much, you'll get indifferent results.
3 Work with a friend or mentor to identify reasons why your particular mix of skills and experience can help you stand out.
4 Your online profile and any other published, printed or emailed information about you contributes to the overall picture.
5 Find out what you are already known for before adjusting the picture.
6 If you hope to be recommended, plan the three pieces of information you want to come up in conversation.
7 You refer people when you have evidence that they can do the job. You recommend them when you're prepared to put your own reputation on the line.
8 It's your job to shape and control the messages about you that form your market reputation. If you don't, you leave them to chance or misunderstanding.
9 Be honest about how much fear of failure gets in the way of taking even small, easy steps.
10 Throwing yourself directly at the outcome of influencing people is often counterproductive.

5

Face time

This chapter helps you to:

- Appreciate the power of face-to-face meetings
- End the habit of hiding behind screens and connecting at a distance
- Learn how a casual mention can become a heartfelt recommendation
- Ensure that you have real, relationship-building conversations
- Avoid getting locked down by false modesty

Why face to face matters

There's a wonderful phrase kicking around the Internet at the moment: 'a handshake beats a signature'. I haven't been able to trace its origin – it probably comes from cultures where someone's word is valued more than a written contract. It's also a healthy reminder that at times things only happen when you look someone in the eye.

Think of friends or colleagues who have made interesting breakthroughs in the past year or two – exciting new clients, brilliant contacts, an engaging new job or work project. Ask them how the opportunity happened. Some will tell you that opportunities fell into their lap, or they were 'in the right place at the right time'. You may feel your friends have talent or luck on their side, but other factors are also at play. Consciously or not your friends did something different to move luck in their direction. They spent less time staring at screens, and more time in face-to-face conversations.

As this book has shown, breakthroughs happen through people exerting influence on your behalf, and they only do that when they move from being a contact to being someone who has a relationship with you. And it must be obvious that warm, effective relationships are built through good quality conversations and rarely secured by email – even more rarely by texting. They sometimes happen as a result of telephone 'meetings', but breakthrough moments are infinitely more likely to happen when the conversation is in person.

Why are lucky breaks more likely if you have met someone in person? Two reasons: trust, and memory. Trust isn't available on demand. It needs to be built, cultivated, appreciated. As negotiators and deal-makers have known throughout history, the best way to build trust is to sit down with someone and share time, small talk, refreshments, perhaps a meal.

Memory is equally important. How long do you remember an email? Sometimes for no longer than 90 seconds. And a telephone call? Typically for half a day or so. Conversely, how long do you remember a warm, interesting face-to-face meeting? It could be several years, particularly where someone follows up with a thank-you note explaining why the conversation was helpful. Real conversations stick in the memory. If the conversation means you keep in touch you'll remember it forever.

Hiding behind screens

The electronic communication tools at our fingertips are phenomenal. The Internet represents a magic combination of history's most comprehensive reference library and most effective detective agency. You can track down opinion, facts and people in seconds; trying to get well-tested opinion, objective facts and the right people takes rather longer.

The mistake is to believe that because something is fast and easy, it's also the best tool for all tasks. Social media can be a great way of keeping in regular contact with people you've known for a long time, where offline and online conversations blend. There is of course a distinction between people you already know well, and those acquaintances and strangers who drift into your orbit if you have an online presence. If you say enough interesting or controversial things on Twitter, you'll get a following. You get similar results through activity on Facebook and LinkedIn. Social media is good for rapidly making connections, but many will remain low-commitment unless you make a stronger bond.

Social media can be a great way of building actual relationships, but only if you ignore the rules of the game. The first rule to challenge is that screen time is useful in relationship building. For some teenagers it's necessary to maintain online activity to maintain social position, but that's not the same thing. Screen life is far less memorable and less meaningful than human interaction. It washes over you, like so much of the day's passing information, and leaves little trace.

Long-distance relationships are sometimes effective, but we frequently use electronic channels to avoid face-to-face encounters. Using email to maintain distance is more than reluctance to step into someone's office or pick up a phone – it's an attempt to avoid the awkwardness and demands of real conversation. You send an email when you could just walk down the corridor. You ask a question online to a community when you could ring someone who has all the answers. You try to hop from one connection to another using LinkedIn alone when picking up the phone produces quicker results. Electronic connecting feels easy, but it keeps people at arm's length, and adds to the risk of striking the wrong tone.

In, out and forwarded

When you receive information, you do something with it. Most of it is forgotten immediately, especially in the modern world where you are bombarded with facts, opinions and requests all day. However, some information is retained, and some acted upon. Reasons vary. Clearly, if your boss gives you a high-priority task you're unlikely to forget it or the details of what you're required to do. Some information you act upon because repeating it becomes a way of entertaining others – jokes, good stories and gossip.

Look at email as an analogy. Some messages get trashed on receipt, some are half-read and largely ignored, others demand your full attention and some kind of a response. This could be a reply, but perhaps you might forward a message to someone who will benefit. This could be because it's information worth sharing, someone needs to be in the loop on an issue, or it could simply be because you're passing on something that will spark someone's curiosity. Some of the most interesting emails begin 'I read this and I thought of you...' which of course is a far better relationship-builder than a plain, abrupt 'FYI'.

Memory, choice and action

Chapter 4 revealed how people remember a small number of things about you. Why might someone remember anything at all? What would prompt them to pass something on? Think about what gets filtered out, but think also about what stays filtered in. You might think the answer is to have a snappy one-liner or a distinctive offering, but none of this matters if you haven't given your contact a reason to remember you.

Start with your own experience as a listener. When some-one talks to you about their work, the same editing and fil-tering processes apply. Instinctively you 'tag' things people say into different categories. Some words are forgotten as soon as you hear them because they seem boring or irrelevant. Other material 'sticks' because it's interesting, entertaining, unusual or colourful. You remember some facts, but you're more likely to remember a story, an analogy, a good turn of phrase. Retention is often unconscious, but you make conscious decisions about what to note down. Sometimes you make that decision while the person is with you, perhaps making a note on the back of their business card. You also make decisions about the informa-tion you will pass on.

Conscious self-projection is rather different to random con-versation because you *plan to be remembered*. Being polite to a fellow commuter has social value, but if you want to form a longer-term relationship you need to give someone a reason to stay connected to you. Having a valid reason to stay in touch means it's much easier to reach out to someone again. Being remembered is vital if you hope someone will do something on your behalf, particularly a recommendation.

Physically placing ourselves in front of people is a wonder-ful antidote to the information age. In a digital world we try to manage relationships through screens, as if determined to forget what an exciting and effective conversation feels like. Yes, some face-to-face encounters don't linger much in memory, but that's only if the impact level is low.

Meaningful connections

Talk to people about their best moments in work, and they'll usually say something about people. These stories are usually about real interactions, not conversations at a distance. This could be about delighting a customer, working in a great team or being in the presence of a visionary leader. Some talk about receiving support from a mentor, or the satisfaction of passing on skills and wisdom to an apprentice. Interestingly, they often talk about moments of trust and appreciation.

One of the best ways of being remembered is to ask for help (*see also* Chapter 9). Experienced professionals treasure moments where they have made a big difference to someone. These stories often begin 'I don't normally take this kind of meeting' or 'the request was so cheeky/charming/funny/sincere, how could I say no?'. Drill deeper and you'll hear about a response to someone who openly sought help (and did some homework in advance). Some will tell you of the warm 'thank-you' card kept safe in a drawer. The pleasure of helping someone and being thanked in return is a special kind of cement when it comes to building relationships.

The pause and the script

It's always interesting to hear the reasons people give for being unable to make connections. Don't know anyone? Chapter 8 deals with that one. The other big barriers are 'I don't want to look stupid' or 'I don't know what to say'. Both comments are clear indicators that you've got the wrong kind of person in mind for a starting conversation.

Don't just hope for referrals, ask for them politely. Then – to avoid approaching people cold – ask for warm introductions and you'll get them. This means being completely open about next steps. Ask 'who else do you think I should talk to?'. When a name comes up, say honestly 'I hate ringing people out of the blue, so could you kindly ring ahead and explain to your colleague why I'd like a conversation?' Setting things up so you never have to say 'You don't know me, but…' is a vital step in moving quickly through the various stages of relationship building (*see* the Zone System in Chapter 10).

Watch for that deadly pause when you are about to dial a phone number. Hesitation is a clear indicator that you are trying to have a more risky conversation before mastering the basics. When you ring someone you know well and feel relaxed with, you don't need a script. You'll just dial and say 'Hi, it's me'. When calling someone where you feel unsure of yourself, you'll probably run a short script in your head first. It often begins 'I'm ringing you because...'. Scripts can be useful (*see* the Appendix), but if you're constrained at an early stage by worrying about what you will say, that's a strong indicator that you're taking things too fast.

Look close by

Most of your initial contacts are close by – not necessarily in terms of location but within your immediate reach. These are probably people you have met personally over the past few months. Don't exclude social connections. Too many people imagine that their perfect contact is a long way off and they waste time and confidence approaching people cold when good connections are one easy phone call away.

In Chapter 10 you'll be introduced to gradual steps forward. Your initial discussions will be with people you already know and trust. You don't have to have an agenda apart from trying things out and moving forward into other discussions. Later exchanges will be about information and influence, but early conversations are good opportunities for learning to talk about yourself.

Becoming a people watcher can provide a range of strategies that could work for you. Listen to the way strangers talk to each other on trains and planes, especially if your normal preference is to bury your nose in a book. People rarely boast or score debating points – they look for areas of mutual interest. Good conversationalists ask questions as well as volunteering information. When people part at the end of a journey they sometimes swap phone numbers. People are connecting all the time, and the conversation doesn't begin with 'I want you to help me' but usually with 'I hope you avoided the rain...'!

Finding the right middle ground

Kick out the assumption that you'll either become an in-your-face networker or you'll give up the whole idea. It's easy to believe that if you can't sell yourself there's no point seeking meetings. It's not a question of two polar opposites: 'hard sell or no sale'. It's about finding a style that you find relatively easy and comfortable with (you'll still have to put some work in) but one that works – things happen because of what you say. Connecting with people makes new things happen. So avoid the alternative – sitting in silence staring at a computer screen, hoping that email and social media will open the right doors.

Think about 'in your face' networkers (*see* Chapter 8). What do they do that is so irritating? As we've established, they talk about themselves a lot. And, because they have been coached to be explicit about their achievements and talents, they're immodest. To be effective they believe it is important to be explicit about their strengths, skills, personal qualities and the high points of their careers. Think of the listener's perspective. How interesting is it to hear someone say 'what I'm really good at...' or 'my strongest skill is' or 'the reason people ask for me is...'? It easily becomes an ego trip with you as a trapped audience. What's in it for you? Why should you continue listening?

The next time you feel the need to impress, ask yourself if you'd be better off listening for longer. Make the most important outcome of the conversation the opportunity to get to know the other person. Ask about their experience and background. How did they get into their current role? What's changed since they entered the sector? Who's doing exciting work? What are their thoughts on the future of the industry?

Modesty and trumpet blowing

Along with the advice to 'get out there', if you're more reserved you may also feel badgered by the phrase 'blow your own trumpet' – in other words, if you're not loud and proud then no one will step in on your behalf. Many people don't operate this way. Trumpets are used for military signals, triumphant entries, fanfares. They're about noise, not subtlety.

The subtext behind the injunction to blow your own trumpet is that you must avoid the great sin of modesty. It's fair to say that large parts of our culture equate the word 'modest' with 'self-effacing', 'timid' or even 'weak'.

A suspicion of modesty was not always part of our society. In the past an individual's character was often held as far more important than their achievements. In the 21st century, Western culture sees extrovert behaviour not just as the best way of doing business, but as an indication of inner strength. As Chapter 1 outlined, this feels very alien to some other cultures. Some cultures expect individuals with significant skills or intelligence to stand out visibly, others instil a reluctance to do so – the 'tall poppy syndrome' suggests that it's sometimes counterproductive or even dangerous to stand out from the crowd.

Blow your own trumpet? Here again significant numbers of the population are receiving advice that they can't take on board. If you're an introvert you nod, agree and silently vow to do nothing of the sort. Modesty can arise from self-esteem issues; quietness is about consciously and reflectively moderating your impact on others. Modesty can mean discomfort responding to praise and an unwillingness to claim personal success. Modesty can be attractive, but can prevent others understanding how useful you can be. Many employers enjoy having introverts in the workplace, but they also say that these people are often unwilling to talk about their abilities at interview, which blocks their path to a job offer.

'Underplaying achievements is almost like a sport in Britain. Pay a compliment and people will say – "Oh, I didn't do anything. Anyone could have done that. It didn't take much." Owning up to your talents is the first step to building a reputation.

Next time someone pays you a compliment, pay close attention to what they say and thank them. Honest, positive feedback is precious and powerful: it helps you grow your reputation based on what others truly value about you, and not on what you think matters.'

Ruth Winden, social media expert & career coach

Thankfully, there are other ways of behaving that are effective – and true to your own style if you're not inclined to sing your own praises. Rather than getting into the either/ or game of modesty versus self-promotion, learn the conversational tricks that allow you to talk about yourself without embarrassment. Many are coming up in the chapters ahead (including authentic connecting in Chapter 7, plus Connection Statements in Chapter 14). Discover ways of talking about what you find exciting rather than talking about what you do.

How do I know if it's working for me?

Look at it from the perspective of someone with a problem. A task needs to be completed, a solution provided, a project led. How do you fix the problem? You ask for a recommendation.

From the smallest task to a job you want to fill, your first instinct will probably be to ask around. So flip that round to the perspective of the individual hoping to be noticed, promoted, seconded, hired.... If you're in that situation, how do you know when your programme of influencing, outreach and self-projection is working? There is one clear measure of success: your name comes up when you're not in the room, and the right things get said.

Even in a high-tech age, most high-value referrals happen in conversation. It's important to remember that nearly all of this happens in your absence. You're not standing just outside someone's field of view, urging someone on, giving them the thumbs-up when you hear something you like. On the contrary, most important communication about you happens when you are not around to confirm or correct. At best, your name comes up in a sentence which describes the kind of problems you love to solve.

This isn't a matter of chance. When people say 'I was lucky – I had a phone call out of the blue', this is usually the kind of luck they have shaped for themselves. People only talk about you if they know about you, and the right actions are prompted by the right messages. Tell people what floats your boat. Tell them what kinds of projects or connections you're looking for. When describing what you do, talk about a mix of ingredients in a role rather than using job titles.

Top 10 messages from this chapter

1 Face-to-face encounters matter – pretending otherwise just puts the handbrake on communication. Face-to-face discussions also help you discover far more.

2 Adopt the habit of 'getting in front of people' rather than communicating from a distance.

3 Work harder at being remembered, rather than just wanting to make an initial impact.

4 Bend social media in your direction so that it leads to real meetings rather than just electronic links.

5 People enjoy helping others – especially if they're asked to deliver something in their gift.

6 Avoid approaching people cold as they feel you are going to ask them to do something they will find uncomfortable.

7 The most important information about you travels outside your direct influence – people talk about you.

8 Don't be hamstrung by modesty; find a more natural style of showing how your achievements may be relevant to others.

9 People recommend others based on relationships of trust, which begin with conversation not information.

10 Recommendations are less about luck and more about the relationships you build and the messages you project.

6

Take the focus off yourself

This chapter helps you to:

- Understand why networking conversations are often mishandled
- Avoid the dangers of planning and reflecting too much
- Seek out conversations, not captive audiences
- Learn the first steps towards a more natural communication style
- Avoid trying to impress with bland statements about your personal values

What gets in the way?

Meeting people professionally feels effortless to some. Others worry about sounding needy, or worry about what to say. You can probably remember moments when you felt tongue-tied or like a rabbit in the headlights. Thankfully, these are rare – in everyday exchanges expectations are not all that high. If you're chatting at a conference and something comes out a bit stilted, people probably won't notice or care. Most people have a reasonably high degree of tolerance for shyness and embarrassment – you may be beating yourself up for behaviours that have hardly registered.

Be honest about the part of the process that feels hardest for you. It might be picking up the phone to someone who's expecting your call, or generating the energy to go to an event even though you have a ticket. Some tasks feel even tougher, like summoning up the courage to walk up to someone at a conference and begin a conversation.

'Whenever I get nervous about making a first contact (and I still do!), I think of three things: (1) When I was at my best. Where was I? I transport myself back to that time and place to rekindle the good feelings. (2) When did someone last thank me for a good deed that I performed? Again, I temporarily bask in that pleasant memory. (3) I remember that I'm only required to be in role for the short-term, after which I can return to my preferred style. Like all good actors, I rehearse my lines and think about what the other "actor" might say in reply. I then plan a tangible reward to give myself once the task is completed. This can be as simple as a cup of tea or a bar of chocolate.'

Darryl Howes, strategic business networking specialist

Watch for two things that can seriously get in the way.
 Two rules for talking about yourself:

1 Don't spend more time thinking, anticipating and pro-cessing than you spend talking to other people. This is the danger of **over-processing**.
2 It shouldn't feel like it's all about you. This is the danger of **self-focus**.

Over-processing

One of the important things that gets in the way of relaxed, effective chat is the conversation you're having with yourself. Think about the last time you felt that you 'let yourself down' in a conversation. You may have thought about it a dozen times afterwards. That's what self-talk is like – it loves repetition. First of all you beat yourself up for saying something embarrassing – or not saying anything at all. Then you beat yourself up for what you should have said. The French expression *l'esprit d'escalier* (literally 'staircase wit') describes the witty retort you think of on the staircase after you've left the room. It is usually accompanied by a feeling that things would have gone so much better if you'd had the right words available at the time. Reflecting on past conversations once or twice can be a good learning experience, but self-talk easily becomes a repeated cycle, and it's time to move on.

Over-processing can apply to the future as well as the past. You may over-think what you're planning to say and when you speak your words sound clumsy. Practising more and thinking less will help, as you'll discover below.

Talking to other people in a relaxed way begins with feeling more at ease with who you are.

'It's surprising how many persons go through life without ever recognizing that their feelings toward other people are largely determined by their feelings toward themselves, and if you're not comfortable within yourself, you can't be comfortable with others.'

Sydney J. Harris, US writer

Self-focus

As soon as you get the idea into your head that it's important to influence and be remembered, it's easy to forget that the medium is a conversation. As earlier chapters outlined, some people go into full-on sales mode, or just talk too much. One result can be apparently endless self-projection, speaking rapidly and at great length. The cause may be arrogance. Where people like listening to themselves, the only person whose needs are being addressed is the one delivering the monologue. More commonly it's a nervous impulse to fill silence, or a vague hope that if you bombard people with a hundred pieces of information, something will stick.

It's all too tempting to over-project

'These days everyone with a LinkedIn account – which means pretty much everyone – is a self-proclaimed expert, thought leader, trendsetter, or influencer. It's no secret that I find that sort of self-absorbed self-promotion to be self-serving, not to mention incredibly annoying and occasionally nauseating ... Nobody wants to work with a self-interested, self-absorbed, self-serving self-promoter. Nobody. If you think about it, neither would you.'

Steve Tobak, founder of Invisor Consulting

When subjected to a full-on broadcast, your attention drifts. On the phone you stop listening and start to check your email. Face to face, you find an excuse to move away. The art of conversation is about being entertaining and generous. You're like a good host, relaxing a guest by encouraging them to join the discussion. It's much more enjoyable to discuss shared interests than to listen to people describe themselves. One-sided discussions can feel entirely transactional. There's a deep irony here. *Conversations designed to project you out into the world work better if they feel as if they are about the other person.*

Persuading people to support you without getting in their faces

With family and friends, some conversations are balanced, some are one-sided. If you're visiting an aged relative who lives on her own, she'll probably want to talk your socks off. In professional conversations an imbalance feels much more noticeable. At a training event, for example, people want to learn but they also want to ask questions to apply learning to experience. At conferences we expect to meet people we don't know, and when we do we expect to speak as well as listen. There's almost an acknowledgement of the artificial nature of such conversations. We go to such gatherings to be able to offer and receive small bursts of information, and not getting enough chances to speak leaves us feeling short-changed.

Reaching out to strangers through social and professional networks should never be about unburdening yourself. People who have too much to say about themselves often sound as though they are using conversations as a form of therapy, seeking affirmation or reassurance. There can be a place for seeking support (*see* Zone 1 in Chapter 10), but remember the importance of leaving the right total impression – 'helpful' trumps 'needs help' every time in this context.

First steps towards a more natural conversation

Opening gambit

This phrase describes a tactical chess opening where a piece is risked to gain advantage. The phrase comes from a 1650s Italian term for a wrestling move: *gambetto*, literally 'a tripping up'. The term also describes a way of starting a conversation without falling on your face.

What can you say as a conversation opener? Avoid anything that sounds direct. Approaching someone saying 'Who are you and what do you do?' sounds arrogant. Keep it short, uncomplicated, light rather than serious. Say things that prompt an answer. Talking about the shared environment is easy and appropriate – travel, weather, qualities of the building. Don't sound downbeat or glum, as this provides a negative first impression. So 'challenging weather, eh?' is better than 'isn't it dreadful?'

Positive openings set the tone for the next few minutes. One of the best ways of sounding positive is to feel positive, which is easier to achieve than you might imagine. Richard Wiseman's *Rip It Up* provides exercises anyone can do to feel positive. The next time you join a refreshment session at a conference, verbalize to yourself quietly, out of earshot, how much you're enjoying the day, the speakers, the venue, and then start a conversation. Just keep saying 'I'm enjoying this... it's really good'. We despise positive psychology for being painfully obvious, but it works.

Pay attention to the way other people start conversations with you. Sometimes people reveal that they're happy to edge towards a slightly more serious discussion. Many observe the social courtesy of asking a question before offering information, or they wrap them together: 'I'm finding this really interesting. How about you?'

Second base

OK, you've exchanged initial thoughts about the weather, the setting, the talk you've just heard. What next? This is where things can get sticky. An awkward silence at this point can be decoded as 'I'm not sure I want to take this conversation any further'. Keeping things going needs just a little injection of energy and interest.

A few stock questions come in handy, but the problem with such questions is that they can sound half-hearted, naive, oddball, or like an interrogation. I've had people ask me 'What's your main objective being here today?' – which feels like someone completing a customer survey questionnaire. If after a presentation you demand 'tell me three things you enjoyed about that talk, and why' you'll probably raise an unwelcome laugh.

Say one thing about what's just been happening, briefly and in an upbeat tone. If you begin with a negative you're in danger of sounding harsh or pessimistic. Think of a tennis player, bouncing the ball first and then serving it. You're going to make one comment and then put the ball into the other court; tack a question on to the end of a brief statement:

Bounce and serve

- 'I'm here to find out more about X. Useful isn't it? What brings you here today?'
- 'I'm finding this stuff really practical. How does it help your line of work?'
- 'This is all new to me, but really interesting. How about you?'
- 'This material fascinates me. What's your take on it?'
- 'I'm already thinking about how I can put this into practice next week. What about you?'

Do you object to the way these examples are worded? Excellent. You're half way to finding your own language and phrasing.

Keeping things going – don't just wait for your chance to speak

Once you've got the conversation started, keep it going. It's like lighting a fire, adding kindling one piece at a time until the fire burns without your help. Keep asking open questions, listening and encouraging further contributions:

The 5 Secrets of keeping conversations going

Seek – more detail

Summarize – a quick recap often helps to show you're paying attention

Share – one or two things about yourself that mirror the other person's experience

Show – your interest, enthusiasm, curiosity, what you've already discovered

Suggest – a reason to keep connected and continue the conversation.

Rehearsed spontaneity

Why do some forms of conversation sound more natural? Being advised that you need to sound 'relaxed' can also press your guilt buttons – why doesn't this come easy? Surely all you have to do is to stop working so hard and start to behave normally? In Chapter 1 we looked at the near-useless directive to 'just be yourself'. Which version of yourself? – We have multiple selves available depending on mood and confidence level.

If you know anything about the work of the best comedians and public speakers, you'll know that they spend huge amounts of time rehearsing material and timing so that it sounds improvised and fresh. Mark Twain famously wrote: 'It usually takes me more than three weeks to prepare a good impromptu speech.' Great performers know how to make a rehearsed line sound ad-lib, how long a pause should be, even what they will say if they are heckled.

This is brilliant news for the rest of us, because it shows that you can rely less on instinct and more on hard work. Think about questions and statements you can try out, practising on your own or with friends. If they sound uncomfortable, that's probably how they sound to others. Adjust phrases until they flow well – until they come to mind as the kind of things you would say. Try using shorter phrases. Make things brief and uncomplicated and they'll begin to sound like normal speech rather than something formal or forced. You might be wondering 'How do I know what sounds natural for me?'. The answer is simpler than you think: it's how you sound when things are going well and you're feeling quietly confident: you – at your best. (*See* also Chapter 7 on what authentic sounds like when it comes to describing your experience and strengths, and 'Starter Script D: Networking Encounters'.)

Listen, and shift the centre of gravity

Great conversationalists who get exactly what they want out of networking conversations are usually excellent listeners. They are instinctively aware of the balance between listening and speaking. If they have been talking for a minute or two, they will ask an open question that signals that they are in listening mode: '... So that's why I'm here. How did you get involved in this project?'

If you want to communicate, listen. Really listen. This advice is everywhere, and yet frequently ignored. Listening has powerful results: people feel that they are important enough to command your attention. They feel, even if you say very little about yourself, that the conversation has been successful. Job interviewers, for example, often say that the interview went very well even when they did all the talking.

Active listening comes from person-centred counselling, which uses Carl Rogers' term **unconditional positive regard**. In counselling that means attending to the needs of the client more than the needs of the therapist. In business conversations it means putting as much attention on building rapport as obtaining information. According to a MIT (Massachusetts Institute of Technology) programme someone who is actively listening 'looks and sounds interested, adapts the speaker's point of view, and clarifies the speaker's thoughts and feelings'.

Real listening is more than shutting up. Genuine listening has two key ingredients: *paying* attention and *showing* attention. Listening isn't enough; you need to show that you're listening. First, be generous with your body language. Nod occasionally, but make sure your face and body are turned directly towards the person speaking to you, not scanning the room for other prospects. Sometimes you will interject small noises or words ('really?' ... 'fascinating...'). Communication experts call these

minimal encouragers, designed to invite further contributions rather than interrupt. Used sparingly they help – used too often they communicate insecurity and a need for approval.

Next time you're talking to a stranger, set yourself a challenge. Imagine your task was to ask a follow-up, probing question at the end of every sentence. To do that you'd listen with enormous care. You'd focus on remembering particular words or phrases that seemed meaningful. You'd frame a question around every piece of information offered. Listen hard for phrases you can pick up on. If someone says 'I've heard this idea before', ask 'Where was that?' and 'What was different about today's talk?'.

When listening saves lives

Some of the most developed forms of active listening can be found in the world of crisis mediation and hostage negotiation. Skilled negotiators are adept at repeating key phrases and paraphrasing, but they also calm the situation, working out what might be unsaid and going on 'under the surface', spotting language that indicates emotional state and unstated intentions. These experts also remind us that talking about listening is not the same as doing it. In 2001 police psychologist Mike Webster found in a study of Canadian law enforcement specialists that, despite extensive training, on average active listening was used only 13 per cent of the time among veteran crisis negotiators.

Communicating values

Strong brands, we're told, demonstrate a blend of consistency and value we call **brand integrity**. If you trust a brand, you assume that it will deliver what it promises. The argument is that if people are like brands, they need to demonstrate and communicate values. This has become a mild obsession. In the past, principles like the **golden rule** (treat others as you expect them to treat you) were working models for the way a whole community might operate. Today, values are very much seen as choices made by each individual.

As human beings, we're naturally inquisitive about how people 'tick', and enjoy the company of individuals who see the world the way we do. Even so, it's a curious idea that people immediately want to hear about your values. It's good to be known for qualities such as honesty and trustworthiness; the problem is in telling other people this as soon as you meet them. You'll hear people say: 'I believe in treating people as equals' or 'I'm a firm advocate for honesty in business' – statements that easily sound shallow.

Organizations do exactly the same thing, using PR channels to tell us about their values. They express pride in developing their staff, valuing their customers and caring for the environment. The problem is that values are easy to claim, harder to put into practice. Some organizations deliver, others do the exact opposite of what they promise – but they all use the same words. We're swamped by so much 'values' language it often becomes meaningless. Politicians try to win votes by associating themselves with strong, abstract terms such as 'accountability', 'public service', 'integrity', 'honesty'. More astute voters ask what candidates will do when they are elected.

People are interested in detail, stories, insights into your working style, not ethical posturing. So take care if you're advised to 'talk about integrity in your elevator pitch'. If you're an introvert it goes against the grain anyway – your natural style is probably to talk about deeper issues only when you know someone well. Forcing yourself to say something like 'I believe in workplace diversity' probably won't feel like you – and that's an instinct you can trust. Elevator pitches using empty value language often make the speaker and listener feel equally uncomfortable.

Beware 'motherhood and apple pie' statements – saying you have strong values makes you sound like everyone else, and sometimes like you're hiding something. If a second-hand car salesman calls himself 'honest Jim', does that mean you automatically trust him? Value claims can make you sound like the new kid on the block (saying on your LinkedIn profile that you're 'hard working' or 'reliable', for example).

Take special care around the word 'passionate'. You might be tempted to say 'I'm passionate about improving the customer experience'. The clichéd term 'passionate about' is now so overused it's become a euphemism for 'moderately interested in'. It can be a form of overselling. It's easier to talk about things that you find exciting, interesting or fascinating. Other clichés can sometimes be just about acceptable. The cliché 'improving the customer experience' might just fly – because it can be linked to tangible change.

Showing beats telling

There's a sound rule about talking about yourself: 'show, don't tell', and it applies here. It's better to give an example than state a fact. Stories are remembered longer than information, and good stories even longer. This is true for describing skills, but even more for personal values. Values are revealed by what you do, not how you describe yourself. Talk about what you've actually *done* rather than spouting abstract values.

Remember that how people see you behave also speaks volumes. Actively listening while networking shows that you really do have an interest in other people. Saying 'integrity is my number one value' is hard to swallow if you've just cut in ahead of someone in the buffet queue. It's curious how many senior managers talk to their mentor about belief in being fair and open – and then spend the rest of the working day disproving the claim.

Top 10 messages from this chapter

1 Be open to improving what you do and overcoming barriers to become a more effective communicator.
2 Self-talk and over-thinking past events can get in the way.
3 Don't waste energy worrying about yourself when it could be better focused actively listening to someone else.
4 Learn how to pitch questions and statements without sounding as though you need therapeutic support or an audience.
5 Listen more, project less.
6 Act as though you might be asked to paraphrase everything you hear.
7 Don't neglect preparation and practice, particularly when it comes to having some good pre-packaged questions for small talk.
8 Be prepared to move the conversation on from gentle chat to something more structured.
9 Keep shifting the focus to what the other person has to say.
10 Demonstrate integrity rather than talking about it endlessly.

7
Authentic impact

This chapter helps you to:

- Organize your curiosity
- Move on from an all-or-nothing strategy
- Sharpen up your social skills and develop a reliable conversation structure
- Seek opportunities for real conversations, not just your chance to speak
- Find a working balance between over-projection and saying too little

Communicating or selling?

This book has looked hard at the advice 'sell yourself'. Does anyone enjoy being bombarded with sales language? Rather than listen to a sales speech, like most people you'd rather talk about what you need – and you're probably wary of being invited to commit to buying before you feel comfortable. Conversations that impress people the most usually involve listening to the other person's experiences. Introverts often say things more thoughtfully and make better listeners, so are generally good at building deeper relationships.

As Chapter 6 shows, it's a huge mistake to believe that the conversations ahead are primarily about you. The focus of the conversation isn't you, but the person in front of you. Organize your curiosity. Plan questions that show genuine interest (and some sound background research), such as 'How did you get into this line of work?' and 'What's changing in this sector?'.

Developing behaviours with more impact

You probably already know how you can improve the way you come across when you meet someone. You may have a long list of things you'd like to improve. Don't try to change everything in one go, but make small changes often. Here are a number of tried-and-tested ways of improving your impact while ensuring that people still feel comfortable talking to you:

SMILING Does your smile seem fixed and fake? How often do you smile? Is it a quick, perfunctory smile?	It's very old fashioned advice, but smiling at people makes them feel attracted to you. Hold your smile for a few seconds. Think about how you would smile if you met someone you're really fond of and haven't seen for a while. That smile makes people feel special.
WHOLE BODY ATTENTION Does your body language convey a different message to the words you're using? Does your posture make you look disconnected, uninterested, ready to move off?	Point yourself squarely towards the person you're talking to so they feel they have your total attention. Lean in slightly as if every word matters.

KEEP STILL Is your body constantly on the move? Fidgeting conveys uncertainty and a sense that you feel inferior to the person you are with. Nervous twitching may also make people doubt your honesty.	Practise keeping still. Stillness, combined with whole body attention and good listening makes someone feel they are at the centre of your world.
SOLID EYE CONTACT Are you distracting someone by looking over their shoulder all the time? Do you look as if you'd rather be somewhere else?	When you meet someone, hold eye contact for a fraction longer than feels comfortable. Return your focus frequently.
WALK AND STAND LIKE YOU MEAN IT If someone sees you across a room, how do they read your posture? Do you look slightly dejected? Sad? Isolated?	Learn to walk tall. Straightening your back, holding your head level and breathing deeper, all contribute to impact.
GET HANDSHAKE FEEDBACK Worried that you immediately put people off with a limp or uncertain handshake?	It's the easiest task in the world to ask a friend how your handshake feels, and practise until it feels positive. Don't crunch bones, but let your muscles show the warmth of your welcome.
LISTEN FOR PROMPTS Don't make the mistake that listening is all about waiting for your chance to speak.	Focus on words and phrases that will keep the conversation going and show you are really listening (*see* Chapter 6).

BREATHE Does your speech come out in an uncontrolled rush?	Slow down and breathe more deeply. It improves your posture and requires you to speak with more gravitas.
PAUSE Don't be afraid of silence, feeling you have to rush to speak every time there's a lull in the conversation.	Pausing for a second or two before you answer a question is usually taken as a sign of thoughtfulness.
VOCAL VARIETY Do you speak quickly, or in a high pitch? Is everything said the same way? Do you show variety in volume, tone and pitch?	Speaking from a deeper register tends to convey authority. Varying tone, pitch and volume makes what you say easier on the ear.
WATCH THE 'NODDIES' Do you use 'minimal encouragers' (*see* Chapter 6) too often? Are you saying 'uh-uh', 'I agree', or nodding too often?	A small amount of verbal encouragement helps, but a constant process of verbal and non-verbal encouragers, including nodding, strongly communicates the idea that you are desperate for the other person's approval.
ENDING PHRASES ON A DOWN BEAT This isn't about saying something negative, but avoiding the modern habit of 'upspeak' – possibly picked up from Australian soap operas – ending every sentence, particularly questions, on an upward inflection.	Practise ending sentences on a downward inflection – it suggests certainty rather than approval-seeking.

SAYING 'THANK YOU' PROPERLY Do you make sure people know they have been thanked? Does your 'thank you' sound automatic or perfunctory?	Thank people with your full attention. Say what you're thanking people for. For example: 'Thank you for making the time to show me around the facility.'
PRAISE Are you making negative remarks about people in your world?	Sniping or sounding cynical often causes you to be remembered as an outsider rather than a key player. Praising people you're discussing, without going over the top, makes a positive tone easy.
DISCLOSE OVERLAP SLOWLY People in need of affirmation tend to point immediately to anything they have in common with their conversation partner.	If you spot something you have in common, ask a few more questions before revealing that you have the same interest.
PREPARE FOR THE PREDICTABLE When asked predictable questions, do you find that the conversation dies after your first answer?	If you're asked where you are from, say something about what's going on there now or why you have moved on. If someone talks about the weather, have a story ready for how it's impacted on you recently.
ASKING ABOUT SOMEONE'S JOB TITLE When you ask 'what do you do?', do you get mixed results?	Seeking job titles is clumsy in a world where people may be self-employed, portfolio careerists, unemployed or home-makers. Ask 'what do you enjoy doing?' or 'how do you spend most of your time?'

TALKING ABOUT YOUR OWN JOB TITLE When you answer the question 'what do you do?', does the conversation falter?	Don't just give a bare job title as it may be of little interest. Develop a short summary of your role such as 'I'm responsible for managing and retaining talent in our organization'.
IMPROVE YOUR RESEARCH Do you find that people are using language – including jargon – that you don't understand?	If you're going to an event where you know people will have a specific interest or you want to build a relationship with someone from an unfamiliar sector, dip into the subject long enough to pick up current language and concerns.

Keeping things REAL

The Appendix provides some working scripts to help you in typical situations. No one likes to be confined to a script, but many people find it useful to work within a structure so they know where they are going. The REAL model reminds you how you progress from initiation to connection.

Keeping conversations **REAL**:

Reach out – initiate a conversation
Engage – make a connection, but keep the conversation enjoyable
Ask – some good questions, which the other person feels comfortable answering
Listen – carefully, with attention, rather than just waiting for your turn

---

Comfortable openings

Conversations, like mighty towers, start small. *See* Chapter 6 on openings. If you jump in by talking about your skills and work experience that will almost certainly be off-putting. Similarly, if you immediately ask probing questions about their sector and organization having just met someone at a conference, then the conversation will conclude quickly.

The trick about work-related conversations, especially in cultures where relationships are everything, is to make the discussion feel as if it's easy, relaxed and as far removed from work as possible. That's why small talk works. Look at the way public figures use it to make people feel valued and important; and skilled negotiators use it at the beginning of a difficult meeting. Talking about the weather, the traffic, the building, sports, hobbies – such typical light, stress-free exchanges help everyone settle down. These topics engage the brain in the gentlest way possible, and in social terms signal 'I am easy to talk to'. Be easy, and the conversation becomes easy.

Stuck for something to say? Small talk is difficult if you think it's irrelevant or trivial. The trick is to be aware of what's going on under the surface – relationship-building. This isn't about friends for life, but warm connections for a few significant moments. People remember the tone of a conversation longer than its content. If you're sitting in a conference hall, talk to the person next to you about their journey, about the weather or traffic. The content matters little, but your conversational opener is really saying 'you look interesting'. Soon you can get to 'what brings you here today?' Chapter 6 outlines a range of methods to begin and maintain conversation.

Practise small talk. Read those three words again. Yes, practise something that seems trivial and so easy to do it's not worth practising at all.

Keep safe, keep positive

Be aware of the different power of positive and negative openings. Saying you're enjoying things is taken as social noise. Saying you're not impressed puts the spotlight on you, potentially suggesting you are negatively critical. There's no need to gush, but saying something positive and constructive about a shared experience is a safer place to begin. So if someone edges up to you at an event and says the coffee and pastries look good, it's safest to agree rather than launch into a diatribe about weak coffee. Criticizing a speech just made by your divisional director may communicate lack of commitment to the organization. Worse still, you may be speaking to the speech writer.

When you really do need to impress

It would be crazy to forget that sometimes you need to take the opportunity and talk about what you do best. Instead of describing your career as if you're the pushiest contestant on *The Apprentice*, try talking about the things you find interesting. 'I'm fascinated by...' is much easier to say than 'I'm good at...'. Telling people how good you are makes you a boring and not very credible conversationalist. You get better results talking about the things you're really curious about. Don't limit yourself to getting across just one thing, either. It's useful to tell people about the range of things that interest you. If you need to name your skills, talk briefly and clearly about your experience and give an example of a recent task. No cheesy one-liners or slick pitch is required, just two or three quietly rehearsed sentences. Don't feel you need to list *all* your accomplishments. You don't have to bombard people with facts, just leave a strong impression of the things you find most captivating – and how someone might help you to take your investigations further.

There are times when you need to talk about how well you do things. It's a good idea to prepare a quick summary of your work highlights, but don't worry about preparing a killer speech (*see* Chapter 3 on the limitations of the elevator pitch). Stay away from phrases that sound like unconstrained egotism, but go for clarity: 'I join up three different groups: innovators and inventors in higher education, businesses, and local authorities. I'm a kind of agent for people with brilliant ideas that they want to patent and take to the market.'

Occasionally, you need to describe what makes you distinctive. Someone might ask 'How do you stand out from your competition?' Or your CEO is standing next to you at the photocopier and says 'what do you do for us?'. The trick is to find the right balance between over-pitching, which is painful to the listener, and under-pitching, which means that shyness or modesty overwhelms you – and people are left with nothing to remember. Don't allow reluctance to be a big mouth to suppress speech altogether.

Talking (briefly) about yourself

- Say something connected to your future, not your past. So not 'I started out as...' but 'I'm trying to find out more about...'
- Don't label yourself unhelpfully, for example by giving a job title that doesn't really capture the reality of your work.
- Avoid singing your own praises until you can do so and feel authentic.
- Don't talk about your strengths yet. Instead, talk about the things that interest you: 'I'm fascinated by...' or 'I'm exploring...'
- If asked, give an example of what you do.

- Mention people, organizations and ideas that fascinate you.
- Don't try to deliver everything in one burst. Say a little, and then turn the conversation around. So if you have talked about your experience, you might ask 'Have you worked in that field?'.

Develop, then practise, authentic language (*see below*). You might start, just for fun, with '*Apprentice*-speak' ('I'm the best office manager on the planet') and then find creative ways of keeping the same energy and yet finding language that works for you. That could be exactly those words, delivered tongue in cheek. It might be: 'I just love keeping our customers and drivers happy by running a well-organized transport office.' Find language that is concise and – if appropriate – explicit: 'I'm probably the most experienced consultant in this field or I'm working with all five of the biggest players in this sector.' Being direct about your market impact often works better when the information is conveyed with humour, being clear that you don't take yourself too seriously. Saying something like 'this is going to sound rather big-headed, but...' can disarm.

Another approach is to begin sentences: 'People say that I...'

'If you find it hard to describe what you do well, consider borrowing other people's words. Weave their descriptions into what you say: "My colleagues have started calling me the IT whizz kid because I am the one who always gets our computers fixed". Or: "What my clients like about my writing is that I can describe complex technical processes in simple terms".'

Ruth Winden, social media expert & career coach

The middle way

Think of the range of TV adverts you see every day. Some are loud, garish and unattractive. You immediately want to hit the mute button. Some people are like that in networking conversations, wanting to get their pitch across at all costs. Other TV adverts are subtle, artistic, heart-warming – but can you remember what products they are advertising? It's important to enjoy the message *and* remember it.

The implied solution is to follow a middle way, but that's a very personal thing. You have to find your own style and voice, which needs to be clear and confident enough to work, but neither false nor irritating.

Two great techniques are also easier than a hard sell. The first is to talk about discoveries you've made, people you've met and interviewed. This shows you are proactive and energized enough to get out there and talk to key people in your target sector. The second is to let your curiosity overflow. Ask lots of questions (smart questions, based on good research). Ask people about their stories rather than always telling them yours. Eventually, carefully, talk about how your stories intersect.

What does authentic sound like?

I do a lot of work with MBA groups in business schools, where you might expect students to have no difficulties in talking about themselves. That's true of the people who speak first and most often, but the ones who queue patiently to ask questions at the end of the talk often say something like 'this doesn't work for me – I can't talk about myself like that'.

As you can tell from the approach taken in this book, I sympathize with this response. Audiences often look liberated when I tell them that self-promotion is often ineffective. However, what you put in its place is what matters. If your strategy is, essentially, 'I can't talk about myself so I will say nothing', that won't work either. Don't start by assuming that you need to say things you find uncomfortable – muttering 'I'm brilliant at...' through gritted teeth.

How do you find a voice that feels authentic to you and sounds it to others? I suggest you talk the way you talk when you're most relaxed. With friends you're far more likely to express interest, curiosity or happiness than to talk about your abilities. If you're pleased with something you've done you will talk about it without sounding vain. You are less likely to say 'I am good at', and more likely to say 'I really enjoyed...'.

AUTHENTIC ALTERNATIVES

If this feels uncomfortable...	Try this...
I am good at...	I enjoy...
I excel at...	I'd love to find out about....
My achievements are...	Something I've got a lot out of is...
I have a great network...	I'm trying to meet people who...
My best skill is...	I've had a great time doing...
I want to be...	I'd love to find out more about...
My strengths are...	I get a buzz out of...
My career goal is...	I'd love your feedback on some of my ideas
What I'd love you to do for me is...	Where should I be looking?
Can you give me a name?	Who else should I be talking to?

So the real alternative to 'selling yourself' isn't to hide away – or to allow yourself to make a mess of every conversation and go home feeling beaten up. You don't have to become someone else or transform what you do. Seek out your authentic voice, and practise using it.

Reflecting on his poem *Digging*, Seamus Heaney wrote:

'Finding a voice means that you can get your feeling into your own words, and that your words have the feel of you about them.'

This applies to speaking as well as writing. Finding your voice means you anticipate real conversations, road-testing language on people you trust (*see* Zone 2 in Chapter 10).

Avoid the temptation to rehearse in high level meetings before you're at ease with your script. Put the work in well in advance. Develop a collection of mini-scripts. Polish and rehearse until they flow unimpeded. Doing the work where it matters means you'll be fully equipped for moments that matter. If you pretty much know what you're going to say in response to predictable questions, you can put your focus on listening and relationship building.

How your working style creates impact

Judging how much to push is about understanding organizational culture, knowing what's acceptable and what's seen as arrogant. In every workplace, some characters are more visible. They're usually the first to speak in a meeting, or the first to grab the flipchart pen. At times they can suppress other contributions. When you start a new role, speaking louder and more frequently than established team members can easily irritate – unless you've been specifically hired to shake up an underperforming team. Good communicators know when to tread lightly, and when to shut up. If you speak most of the time at meetings, seek feedback on how many toes you crush in the process.

You might have the opposite problem and hate anything that looks or feels showy, and find it hard to talk about your contribution. The difficulty is that your competencies only have currency when they are noticed. Always being the last to speak in a discussion can signal lack of interest as well as shyness, and can flag up a lack of leadership ability. Avoiding speaking in public is a great way of not being observed by the managers in your organization who make decisions about people development. If you shun the limelight, you give others permission to ignore your contribution.

Learn how to describe your achievements as simple facts, rather than constantly apologizing or saying 'all I did was...'. Don't fudge or downplay what you have done – tell it how it is. (*See* Chapter 13 to think further about how others see you at work.)

Top 10 messages from this chapter

1 Connecting isn't about selling, but understanding how others see the world.
2 Look at the range of behaviours that improve one-to-one conversations, and start to adopt new habits.
3 Structures help to begin and develop conversations.
4 Plan and practise conversational openings that don't sound forced and put people at ease.
5 Work at comfortable openings that lead to deeper connection.
6 Make sure you know how to move into the second phase of a conversation.
7 Learn active listening rather than simply waiting for your chance to talk.

8 Practise talking about what inspires you rather than what you think you're good at.

9 Don't use high level conversations for first-step rehearsals.

10 At work, think about your overall impact, not just how you talk about yourself.

8

New rules for networking

This chapter helps you to:

- Learn a new way of connecting to people
- Gain insights into why people dislike certain kinds of networking approaches
- Change your language and mindset, and then take micro-steps towards new behaviours
- Focus on quality rather than quantity in connections
- See how an effective structure can help your conversations

Looking at what gets in the way

What do you hate most about being a networker? Here's what people say in answer to that question:

Reasons why I don't believe networking is the right thing for me

- It's unfair – people should be given opportunities because of their ability, not who they know.
- It makes me look desperate.
- It feels like begging for favours – asking a lot and giving nothing back.
- It requires influencing skills that I don't have.
- Only smooth operators with glib elevator pitches succeed.

Reasons why I can't start networking

- I don't know what to say about myself – it ends up sounding fake or immodest.
- I don't have anyone I can approach.
- I hate cold calling people.
- I hate networking events.

... or sometimes you start and then give up:

Reasons why I (secretly) intend to stop networking

- Asking questions makes me look as though I don't know what I'm doing.
- I hate the feeling of not knowing what to say.
- I ask a couple of questions and then dry up.
- I've used up all my contacts.

It all feels a bit tacky...

When someone says that networking makes them feel 'grubby', research suggests that this is not just a metaphor but a genuine physical response. In a study published in December 2014 the authors Tiziana Casciaro, Francesca Gino and Maryam Kouchaki found:

'professional networking increases feelings of inauthenticity and immorality – and therefore feelings of dirtiness – much more than networking to make friends'

'The Contaminating Effects of Building Instrumental Ties: How Networking Can Make Us Feel Dirty' in Administrative Science Quarterly.

The study recorded that those networking for professional reasons often felt 'unclean' as a result; one person reported using large amounts of hand sanitizer after attending business dinners!

On the positive side, the research suggested that feeling unclean diminishes when people network regularly and think about what they put in as well as what they take out.

'If you keep an open mind and see it as an exchange of knowledge it becomes a much less selfish exercise,' writes Francesca Gino, adding that if individuals are 'other oriented' and have a genuine sense of curiosity about the person they talk to, networking becomes a more satisfying experience.

'It will help you feel better in the process because you are not driven by your own selfish goals.'

Francesca Gino

Networking and those who suffer it

Picture a scene you've probably experienced. You're at a conference taking coffee between seminars. A new face looms towards you: a gleaming smile, a firm handshake, a business card is offered. Two sips of coffee later you're being bombarded with a speech: 'Let me tell you about what I do and what I'm looking for. I started 12 years ago in pharmaceutical sales, and....' You discover a sudden interest in emptying your bladder before the next session – anything to get away from the in-your-face networker pinning you into a corner. How do you feel when subjected to a networking ambush?

How we feel when hearing a networking speech:

- I like to meet new people, so that's OK.
- I don't really listen; I just wait until I can speak.
- It takes up valuable time.
- It feels like someone is making a sales pitch.
- It feels like I'm being used, possibly exploited.
- I'm being asked to do something I don't feel comfortable doing.

- It's boring. I have to listen to things that are irrelevant to me.
- The speaker doesn't seem interested in what I have to say.
- I'd rather have a conversation where I learn something useful.

These kinds of responses are typical. We don't like being 'net-worked at' any more than we like being 'sold to'. It can feel like a one-way conversation and a waste of time. Bearing in mind how *you* feel when someone pins you into a corner, do you really want to mimic this behaviour? Is it worth summoning up the courage to operate like this?

You *are* going to have to stand in front of people at key stages of your career, whether this is about getting promoted, seeking development opportunities, finding clients or generally oiling the wheels of working life. However you can learn to do this very differently.

Rethinking the way you connect and communicate

Change your viewpoint

If you hate networking, call it something else. Call it 'catching up with your friends'. Call it 'meeting interesting people'. Call it 'adding to my Christmas card list'. Valuing the people you aim to reach is important. You're not exploiting them, especially if you pay for coffee or lunch and show as much interest in them as you expect them to show in you. Starting with close friends and contacts means you don't have to work hard (*see* Zone 1 in Chapter 10). Friends will also tolerate sudden changes of direction in the conversation and poor questions. As you progress, regularly see people who keep you thinking positively. These contacts will, if you ask, remind you of your strengths and will be positive about moving forward.

While networking some individuals seem to mourn the absence of deeper connections. Small talk can seem superficial compared to meaningful conversations. Devora Zack, author of *Networking for People Who Hate Networking*, suggests that extroverts 'collect' and introverts 'connect' – extroverts network to attract a large number of contacts, while introverts prefer to have a small number of close relationships. In fact, introverts can learn to value the activity as a way of getting to know people really well and to share experiences on a deeper level – so the reason for making a connection is the connection itself. Seeking quality rather than quantity may feel like a more valid reason to begin. Don't feel you have to fill your scorecard with hundreds of conversations. Making time for people starts with making time to find the right people. For you this might be about finding individuals on a similar wavelength who will value the opportunity to meet you. Don't rush to fill your address book. Give relationships time to develop – and people space to discover you're someone they can trust.

Small victories

If you're shy or fear rejection, keep talking to people you know until you gain the confidence to break into new territory. Put some old misconceptions to rest: actively trying to reach people isn't about begging for crumbs from someone's table or exploiting everyone you know. You don't need to have a full contact book. Networking isn't about wealthy or 'old school tie' connections, or only for managers or self-promoters. It's about expanding your horizons, meeting new people, and making sure they remember positive news you choose to broadcast. It's not about being part of an elite club. It's about honestly asking for help that others are usually happy to provide.

Start by picking up the phone to someone you have no hesitation in calling. If you like, begin 'this is going to sound a little strange...' or 'I'm going to get this wrong, but...'. Approaching supportive people means mistakes rarely matter, as the Zone System in Chapter 10 will show you. Friendly contacts have your interest at heart, so they're tolerant enough to cope with mistakes and reversals. Be direct about what you need: a pep talk, some ideas for a presentation, a recommendation, a connection. Being open about outcomes dismisses any sense that you're only pretending to be sociable to wheedle out useful business information. Taking mini-steps means avoiding setbacks, like the cold rebuff you receive when you phone saying 'you don't know me, but...', or when you approach high level contacts too early (*see below*).

Soft structure

Using the system outlined in Chapter 10, start small – spend the first month or so talking to people who are encouragers, asking them questions you've never asked before – about people they know. Try this with friends, neighbours, even family – you'll be surprised at the great connections they come up with. Add structure as you progress. Next time you meet a friend for coffee, plan some questions and think about what would make a good conversation great. Ask for help describing your strengths and what makes you distinctive. Talk about what you're looking for and the kind of people you would like to meet. Don't go home without asking the question 'Who else should I be talking to?'.

Never underestimate the number of people you can reach in just a month or two. US sales guru Joe Girard is famous for his 'Law of 250':

'Everyone knows 250 people in his or her life that they can influence with their opinions and experiences.'

Girard based that figure on typical attendances at funerals and weddings. Other commentators suggest that social media can easily connect us to at least 500 people, but let's accept Girard's rule of thumb. His suggestion is simple: for every person you influence, they can influence 250 more. You can end up with staggering totals. I often start – I ask clients to name just three people they promise to call in a week, who will be each recommend three more. It's a stretch, but not a huge one. Within five rounds of discussions you've easily got approaching 250 people on your call sheet.

Watch out for setbacks, though – the system doesn't work all the time. Sometimes you draw a blank, sometimes people are too busy. If you run out of people to speak to, check your technique. You're probably forgetting to ask people to hand you on. Arranging clear, helpful introductions means the next person in the chain knows what kind of help you need, and is reassured that you're not asking for too much. Ask people for information or insights which are fairly easy to deliver. Tell people as you go along that your plan is to have conversations with a range of people – that way introductions happen naturally. *See* Chapter 15 and the Appendix for ways of starting easily, with a script for your first conversation. When the conversation inevitably turns to you, offer a quick, rehearsed, two or three sentence message that is clear and enthusiastic (*see* Chapter 7).

Beginning a simple but effective networking conversation

1 Be open about the fact that you're asking for help.
2 Emphasize that it's only a small amount of help, easy for your contact to provide.
3 Say that you're talking to a range of people in the sector (this plants the idea that you'd be pleased to receive introductions).

> 4 Be clear that you're not asking for something diffi-
> cult. For example, the conversation is NOT a veiled
> sales call or your attempt to inveigle your way into an
> impromptu job interview.

Big asks

Notice how often the word 'help' appears in this book. Asking
for help is not about weakness, or dependency, and definitely
not about exploiting people. As Chapter 9 shows, cynically
'using' people is clearly counterproductive – it's what people
remember about you, overpowering any other messages you
broadcast. However asking for the wrong kind of help can also
create problems.

Think about how you might respond if asked for help. You
receive an email asking 'can you point me in the direction of
a good website designer?' It's short, clear and will probably get
an instant reply. It's almost easier to answer than to file it under
'to do'. A request for one or two pieces of information is a
smart request because it can be dealt with immediately. However, people often ask for too much, whether they know you
or not. For example, think about the impact of sending a long,
complicated email out of the blue which asks lots of questions. This kind of approach sends unhelpful signals: passivity
(the reader has to do all the work), lack of realism (this person hardly knows you but you're asking for a lot of time) and
clumsiness (it's an intrusion which reveals an inability to 'read'
the relationship). It's almost impossible in a cold email to get
someone to deliver more than one small favour.

So, think about whether you're pitching a micro-request,
which is likely to work, or a 'big ask', which isn't. Let's say you
met someone at a conference yesterday; today you're ringing
to ask for a list of leads. Ask for one lead instead. You might be

tempted to email your CV at this point, not realizing that's an even bigger ask (it takes at least 15 minutes to scrutinize a CV and give proper feedback). Some go even further: 'Please pass my CV on to other divisional heads' asks something professionally difficult. Someone on the receiving end of a big ask will put it to one side – for busy people this probably means it will never be looked at again.

I get emails from people in far-flung countries asking for advice, and they are generally very long letters asking multiple, complex questions, or asking me to do something I can't do. The secret is to ask people for just a little help, and to *ask things people are capable of delivering – with minimal effort.*

The underlying question

Regular networking has extensive, multiple benefits. These aren't chance spin-offs, which is why you might call this method of working **organized discovery**. You become identifiably interested in what's going on, and people start to move information in your direction. You learn a huge amount about target organizations and sectors, picking up insider language – a feel for the way organizations describe success. As a potential business partner you spot organizational needs and problems and pick up on trends and industry news.

To keep focus, *remember the question behind the conversation.* What do you most want to know? At first the question might be 'do you have any ideas?'. Later it's specific: 'who do you know who works in bioengineering?'. As you work through the zones outlined in Chapter 10, your underlying question becomes more focused, especially if you're approaching busy people. The good news is that questions get easier the more often you ask them. With easy contacts, you don't need a well-structured conversation. Frankly, you can mess things up. When it comes to people you've never met before or conversations with senior contacts, the instinct to have a partial script is a good one. It helps to start with an opening statement about why you're pleased to have the conversation, and what your main purpose is. Go for a mix of informal but clear: 'In all honesty, I'm here to pick your brain. I'm trying to speak to a range of people who work in invoice factoring...'

Approaching people at the right time

You might think it makes sense to only approach people who are likely to give you great results. There's some merit in that approach. Aiming for someone who understands what's happening in a work sector is usually a smarter move than talking to someone who is retired – but not always. Don't rule people out, certainly not at the early stages of connecting. Sometimes the most unexpected people give you brilliant results – it's not about their expertise, but the lives they interact with.

Most networkers are interested in reaching decision-makers. It's never easy. These are some of the busiest, most protected people in the world. A better definition of what you're trying to achieve would be *reaching the right person with the right answers at the right time.* Some people believe it's as easy as finding out the name of key staff using Internet research and then writing out of the blue. This can work, but it's rare that even a punchy letter or email gets a response.

Think about including senior and influential people in your networking. They are, after all, people who hold budgets, make hiring decisions, and their recommendations carry more weight. However, be careful of timing. It's unwise but a common mistake is to approach senior contacts at the beginning of your explorations. People decide that they 'should be doing some networking' and they can see the names of one or two VIPs in their contact books. They get the meeting because there is already a connection, but go in unpractised and unstructured.

Usually the impression they create is: 'I'm confused about what I'm looking for and not sure what to say about myself.' This is, quite frankly, a waste of someone's time. It's much better to approach these high-level contacts when you have clear questions, a really focused aim, and something interesting to say about what you're doing at the moment.

Chapter 10 shows you how to build from softer to more demanding conversations. Strength of relationship will often dictate how you move forward. If you already know someone well, all you need do is to pick up the phone. If you know someone only vaguely or don't know them at all it will be smarter to get an existing (lower-zone) contact to make an introduction. Keep asking yourself the question: 'how can I make a connection?' and turn it into a challenge. Search using the company name on LinkedIn to see who you already know, and ask around. You may need to make a quick connection and draw in favours quickly if the need appears urgent or the window of opportunity is closing.

Connecting online

Social media is a great way of tracking people down, particularly if you bend the rules (*see* Chapter 11) and turn online conversations into face-to-face ones at your earliest opportunity. Join LinkedIn groups and make active contributions. Start to build a reputation as an information sharer and subject expert.

'If you find it hard to start a conversation with strangers, whether that's on the phone, a networking event or a conference, use the power of the Internet to find things you have in common. If you need to cold call, research the person's background and plan opening questions in advance. Check out beforehand who else is attending an event and decide who you want to connect with. Then prepare: the more you know about a person, the easier it is to strike a chord, naturally.'

Ruth Winden, social media expert & career coach

If you reach out to people online and ask them to become Facebook friends or connections on LinkedIn, approach the task sensibly. Send some supporting comment when you make a request – something or someone you have in common, or how you know someone's work. When connection requests reach me my question is always a polite: 'Remind me – how have our paths crossed?' It worries me how many people reply: 'I found you on the Internet' or 'LinkedIn suggested that I invite you to connect'. Neither gives me a valid reason to accept.

Keep records of who you've approached, ideally a printed list ready to hand wherever you are in case the phone rings. One technique that brilliantly supports the Zone System is to set out a record of present and future contacts on a spreadsheet. You might use different colours for different zones. Use the sheet to record important contact information but also the notes of previous discussions. Have a column that records your next action – where does each conversation lead you?

Then draw up a spreadsheet listing your target organizations (a list you will probably begin when you have Zone 3 conversations). Your spreadsheet will include the organization name and the names of people you know there. Give each organization a score from 0 to 10. Zero means you know nothing about the organization apart from its name. Five means you know a great deal about what the organization does and you know the names of some people who work there, or have worked there in the past. A score of 8 or 9 means you know the names and job titles of most decision-makers who might be interested in what you have do offer, and you get a 10 if you've had a Zone 7 conversation.

Review your spreadsheet list of target organizations each week and ask yourself what you can do to improve your scores, even by just one point.

Top 10 messages from this chapter

1 Be honest about why reaching out to people feels daunting, uncomfortable or tacky.

2 The idea of networking can provoke powerful reactions, including a sense of feeling unclean or desperate.

3 Think hard about what you hate about being a networking target. Drop these behaviours even if they seem the obvious way forward.

4 If you value deeper relationships, focus on quality rather than playing a numbers game.

5 Take micro-steps, starting low-key and easy.

6 Don't limit yourself just to people you know – you get bigger breakthroughs in new territory.

7 Don't ask too much, or for things that people will find hard to deliver.

8 Begin with an informal but clear statement of why you're asking for help. Use the outline structure in this chapter to help you start.

9 Approach the right people at the right time – don't waste high level contacts by speaking to them before you're ready.

10 Mix online and face-to-face activity to keep generating new contacts.

9
Soft connecting

This chapter helps you to:

- Understand why professional connections are a vital part of your working life
- Learn strategies for reaching people when you lack confidence or connections
- Work, step by step, towards building a community of supportive people
- Learn what to say in easy start-up conversations
- Take small steps to make big things happen

Do I really have to do this networking stuff?

You may be a naturally sociable person. If you already know dozens of people who regularly offer you help, perhaps all you need to do is to keep sharpening up your connecting skills. Many others find that they have only a limited number of people they connect with regularly, and they even struggle to remember why they might want to enlarge this group.

Talk to anyone who has set up a business, switched career paths or set up as a freelancer and they will tell you about the mistakes they made along the way. Ask them one thing they would do differently. A large proportion will tell you: 'I wish I'd started talking to people earlier.' Interestingly, they don't say 'I wish I'd found key people in month one' or 'I should have spoken to the top people earlier' – but they do acknowledge that most of the things they achieved came through talking to people.

This chapter shifts the focus away from how you behave and speak and puts emphasis on (1) how to build support, and (2) what you will end up with. Don't panic – we're keeping things practical and easy – welcome to the art of **soft connecting**. Chapter 2 showed how we frighten ourselves with big thoughts like 'getting out there', 'making an impact', 'selling yourself'. It's possible to begin in a much more low-key way.

Do it as if it isn't about you

Imagine you want to raise funds, lobby for a new school crossing or save a historic building. You decide you need to create, from scratch, a pressure group of about 50 activists. You'd probably write a piece in the local newspaper. A poster seeking expressions of interest might prompt enquiries. You can't mail or cold call because you don't know who might be interested. So you decide to ask people to help you directly. You speak to half a dozen contacts within 48 hours, and within a fortnight a six-person project team sits down for its first meeting. Your team decides to carry on the way you started, by reaching out to individuals. You generate a list of people to approach. But how can you get people on board – quickly and with minimum effort? You could approach each new contact personally, but as they don't know you they might be suspicious and hard to persuade.

Common sense shows how to get maximum leverage in small steps. You ask everyone present to commit to a task. Not a huge task, not something that makes them feel uncomfortable or makes you look lazy. Each team member is asked to set up three conversations – within one week, they are going to speak personally to just three people – face to face. Clearly they're going to target potential supporters – or, at least, people likely to be interested in the topic. Everyone agrees to keep the risk of knock-back low by only approaching people they know well enough to approach without hesitation. You decide on agreed words to explain what the project is about. You coach team-members not to ask 'Are you interested?' (where a 'no' response would kill the conversation), but 'How would you like to help?'. The next stage? Every contact you speak to will be invited to make three new approaches of their own.

Think about how this people machine would work. You would be baffled to hear 'I spoke to three people but they weren't interested'. You'd be surprised if a team member said 'None of my contacts knew anyone else who might be interested'. You'd be stunned if someone said 'I didn't know what to say when I picked up the phone' – simply because the task is so straightforward.

The above strategy shows how you can build a community of interest using three-step thinking:

Building a community of interest – what you need:

1 Your aim is to hear what people think about your project.
2 You also aim to find active supporters.
3 You'd appreciate introductions to people who can deliver on point 1 or 2, or both.

If you ask six people to go out using the three-step approach outlined above, what results could you expect within two-to-three weeks? Feedback, yes – but also ideas for moving the project forward – including the names of new useful contacts. If your project makes sense, soon you'll have at least 50 people onside – without anyone having to say 'you've never heard of me, but I'd like to talk to you...'

Adapting this idea to your individual outreach

This model for building a lobbying group is a good analogy for the way you can do things for yourself. You want to find people who share your interests and values. You don't want to approach people out of the blue. You want to enlist supporters to enquire and lobby on your behalf. You want to be in a situation when the phone rings unexpectedly and it's someone who wants to know more.

When you approach others about your own needs, things don't work so well. You find that you've forgotten why you are making an approach, or you set yourself up to fail by going in cold. You use a script that doesn't work so well. You try to do everything alone rather than enlisting supporters.

Set out to organize self-replicating conversations. This saves time and effort, but it also models what you hope to achieve. Whatever work you do, you want people to be talking about you – and making connections for you – in your absence. You want the phone to ring, or the unexpected email to arrive. Soft networking places your suggestions and questions into the community so that they work unassisted. A goal, plus people, plus delegated tasks, gets the job done.

Do it as if it wasn't for you. How would you network if you were commissioned by a friend to make new connections? You wouldn't go back after a day and a half and say 'I talked to a couple of people but they're not interested'. You'd push hard, push creatively – you wouldn't say 'I checked out that sector and you won't like it' or 'there's no room for someone like you'. No, you'd look, and ask, and keep on asking.

Turn fear into energy you can use

What if it still feels fake or terrifying to approach people who don't know you? Set aside apprehensive thoughts. Turn them into a game.

In Chapter 2 we looked at the work of the Oxford Centre for Anxiety Disorders and Trauma. Professor David Clark has helped subjects to deal with anxiety by reinterpreting bodily sensations in a more productive way – for example, saying to yourself 'exam nerves help focus attention' or 'a little extra adrenaline makes for a better interview'. Psychologist Richard Wiseman draws on this work (*see* 'As If' reframing in Chapter 15), suggesting that we can choose to interpret feelings differently. For example, before a performance review or speaking in public, try saying 'nerves will make sure I'm particularly focused on how my audience is reacting to my speech'. It would be inane to say that verbal reframing changes everything, but the point is that it changes something, and that can be enough.

Soft connecting one step at a time

A three-step approach to soft connecting

The reason soft approaches work is perhaps obvious by now. Otherwise it feels like an uphill struggle, and you'll find reasons to avoid doing it. Starting soft and slow means finding low-risk practice opportunities (use the Zone System in Chapter 10).

Let's go back to our idea of building a community of interest. That's a fairly good way of describing the people out there who will be keeping you in mind. Here's the three-step approach now adapted for your personal use:

Three steps to soft connecting – what I need

1 My aim is to hear what people think (about the market, about who I should be talking to).
2 I also aim to create active supporters (giving me feedback, sharing information, suggesting connections, making introductions).
3 I'm going to ask for introductions to other people who can deliver on point 1 or 2 or both.

Starting from zero

Let's revisit the big question. How do you begin when you don't know how or where? The answer to that question depends of course on who you ask. Some people love networking. They feel it's the easiest, most enjoyable aspect of their work. They never feel they are starting from zero because they generally know who to speak to next, and look forward to the moment. These are some of the people you should connect with first (*see* Zones 3 and 5 in Chapter 10).

Beware entrenched statements: 'I don't have a network.' You declare things in absolute terms under stress ('nothing's working for me today'), and even as you say them you see that they distort reality. The statement 'I don't know any-body' argues a near-impossible condition. Unless you are a home-tutored orphan living on a desert island you really can never be in social isolation. You definitely know some-body, so 'I don't know anyone' really means something else such as:

- I don't know anyone important
- I only know ordinary people who have no influence
- I only know people in my social circle, not work
- I know potentially useful people but I can't possibly approach them
- I've tried speaking to people I already know but it went wrong.

When coaching I leave the absolute statement 'I don't know anyone' unchallenged for about ten minutes, and then ask for the names of three helpful people my client feels able to approach next week. Three names are nearly always forthcoming. If all else fails I might ask 'if you needed an income stream this week to avoid being evicted from your home, who would you talk to?'

Saying 'I don't know anyone important' really means 'I have contacts but I don't think they'll be useful to me'. This suggests that the only kind of people worth talking to are in influential, senior roles. People like this *can* help, enormously, but these people are also very busy and highly attuned to any conversation that seems like a waste of their time. Most people know at least one person like this, but make the mistake of approaching them far too soon (*see* Chapter 8 on approaching the right people at the right time).

How do you choose the right kind of people to begin with?

Who should you talk to first? Classic textbook advice on beginning to network usually invites you to list everyone with whom you have a professional relationship, for example your dentist, vet or bank manager. This is often next to useless. Your bank manager might find it odd if you make an appointment asking for help with your programme of outreach. Many of the professionals within your immediate reach only have a transactional relationship with you.

What kind of people should you reach out to at first? People who are:

- easy to approach because you already know them
- easy to begin a conversation with, because you speak to them regularly
- naturally supportive and prepared to help
- naturally positive and good at coming up with ideas and suggestions
- the kind of people you could go back to more than once, perhaps with different questions or a new approach
- likely to know other people who might help you.

For more, *see* Zone 1 in Chapter 10.

Networking events

You might be wondering if you should be going to events which are, at face value, all about networking. Often these centre on food – breakfast, lunch or dinner. Some people enjoy them, and do well as a result of attending. Who? You guessed it – those who love talking to people. Others often find them the most painful form of networking. Careers specialist Kate Howlett writes: 'Eating soggy croissants at dawn never works.'

The problem with many networking events is that they're full of people who want to talk about their offer rather than to exchange ideas. At a conference you can find both providers and users of services – networking events sometimes only attract providers. You might find synergy and make cross-referrals, but these events seem to work best where someone has a service useful to other local businesses. They're less useful if you're looking for higher level contacts in bigger organizations.

'Today's time-poor work/life environment requires us to adopt a new approach to our networking practices. If we don't, we can spend valuable time attending events and building alliances that fail to deliver on our needs. In effect, we'll end up doing the right things, but in the wrong way. Our start point should therefore be to decide exactly what we want from our networking. How much resource, including time commitment, do we have available to devote to it? What tangible outcomes are we seeking to achieve and is our normal default mode of connecting with people serving us in the best way?'

Darryl Howes, strategic business networking specialist

Online warm-ups

Face-to-face encounters have huge benefits and can be reinforced by online activity. Ruth Winden is an expert in this area:

'Networking is not just about attending large events, networking happens when you connect with people, wherever you are. Sites like Twitter or Instagram make it surprisingly easy to start and nurture business relationships, over distance. You learn so much about people online – what they like, their sense of humour, what they care about. When you eventually meet in 'real life', you'll be surprised how easy it is to connect with someone you've never met before. It's (almost) like meeting a long-lost friend.'

Ruth Winden, social media expert & career coach

Sliding right up to the edge of your comfort zone

Forcing yourself into a networking style that doesn't fit feels like doing something important wearing clothes that make you feel faintly ridiculous. Trying to leap outside your comfort zone feels brave but is often counterproductive. However, thinking 'this won't work for someone like me' means you're ruling out a whole world that you are capable of discovering with relatively little effort. Avoid absolute statements about what you can or can't do, allowing yourself to fall into the 'all-or-nothing' trap. When you hear yourself say 'if I can't put in 100 per cent then there's no point starting', guess which safe, inactive position you're secretly justifying?

As a wise soul once said: 'Most of us are wearing comfort zones several sizes too small.' Find the edge of your comfort zone and operate there for a while – a place where you are stretched but still feel relatively safe. Start by drawing on friends and colleagues – people who will provide feedback, encouragement and information in equal measure, then gradually work outwards. This means following up leads that look interesting, asking around, seeking referrals from friends and colleagues. It means sharing your discoveries, displaying curiosity and enthusiasm, and sometimes catching decision-makers at the point when they have a headache or opportunity that fits what you have to offer.

Borrow some energy

When you're asking questions, focus on subject areas that fire your curiosity. When you talk about subjects you find truly motivating (in comparison with those you think you ought to find out about), it shows in your voice and body language. When you're disconnected from your own words, that shows too – you start to sound robotic and only distantly connected to what you're saying.

Once you find a topic that gives you a genuine 'buzz', you will approach networking with far more energy – something you'll need in abundance. You need energy to keep picking up the phone and persuading people to open doors and create opportunities. Find encouragers who will keep your batteries charged (*see* Zone 1 in Chapter 10).

People remember your self-projection style

Family and friends apply pressure to 'get out there' as fast as possible. So you throw yourself at the biggest hitters you know. What happens? Things start to go wrong. You haven't anticipated how people will respond to you, or questions like 'What exactly are you looking for?' You use up your best connections fast and feel you have no one to talk to. As Chapter 14 shows, the way you hit the market colours your reputation. People remember that you're unsure of yourself or lacking direction – not the kind of messages you want to travel in your absence.

Longer term, people remember *how* you asked for help. If you show curiosity and genuine interest, and if you clearly appreciate the help you're given, people remember – and assume that's your normal working style. They also remember if you're vague, pushy or asking for more than you seem prepared to give back. Commit to a long game, not just short-term returns. Reaching out is about giving and receiving help, not leaving people feeling used.

Richard Nelson Bolles, author of *What Color Is Your Parachute?*, explains why this happens:

'With shrinking time available for nurturing friendships, often we do not approach our friends until we need something from them ...You may not hear from a friend for years, and then suddenly out of the blue they write you to say they are out of work, and they need you to give them job-leads or references or advice or whatever. They took no time prior to this, to make you feel like they value you just as a person, regardless of whether or not you can do anything for them. This trend, in modern times, to neglect our friends until we need something from them, has to be noticed, pondered, and corrected, if we are to be human beings at our best.'

Robert Cialdini's seminal work *Influence: The Psychology of Persuasion* suggests that an important factor in influencing is **reciprocity** – when we receive help, we like to respond in kind:

'Give a positive experience to people and they will want to give you something in return.'

Robert Cialdini, US psychologist

Interestingly, being asked for help makes you favourably disposed to the person who asks for it. It seems that people are more likely to think well of you if you ask for a favour than if you provide one. This is known as the 'Benjamin Franklin effect', based on Franklin's maxim:

'He that has once done you a kindness will be more ready to do you another, than he whom you yourself have obliged.'

Benjamin Franklin, US statesman and political theorist

And as further evidence:

'We all admire the wisdom of people who come to us for advice.'

Sir Arthur Helps, Victorian writer

Research by Katie Liljenquist and Adam D. Galinsky backs this up. They found that asking the other party for advice in a negotiation increases the chance of resolution. In a property negotiation when sellers focused on achieving the highest possible sale price, only 8 per cent managed a successful deal. When they asked buyers for advice, 42 per cent reached a successful agreement. In their 2014 online article they wrote:

'Whether it's a high-stakes monetary negotiation or winning support for a proposal, the simple gesture of soliciting advice can make you more likeable, encourage your counterpart to see your perspective, and rally commitment.'

Liljenquist & Galinsky (2014), 'Win Over an Opponent by Asking for Advice', Harvard Business Review *(HBR)*

Asking for help is open and transparent. US writer Malcolm Gladwell looks at the balance between imposing yourself and asking for help:

'When we talk about people with presence, we often assume that they have a strong personality – that they sweep us all up in their own personal whirlwind ... Presence is not just versatile; it's also reactive. Certain people, we say, "command attention" but the verb's all wrong. There is no commanding, only soliciting.'

Malcolm Gladwell, What The Dog Saw, And Other Adventures

Top 10 messages from this chapter

1 Even low-level, easy conversations will move things forward. Start anywhere, but do start, even if this is online.

2 Adopt the strategies you would use if the process wasn't about you.

3 Work backwards from what you're trying to achieve. How can people help with the intermediate steps?

4 Imagine you were building a community of interest aimed at giving you useful feedback, recruiting active supporters and seeking introductions.

5 Work around internal blocks, such as pretending there's no one you can talk to.

6 Practise with low-level connecting conversations before approaching people where starting a conversation prompts anxiety.

7 Networking events may be the least likely solution to your needs.

8 Find something to get excited about to fire up your questions.

9 Remember that how you interact with people can have long-term career consequences.

10 Build and put work into long-term relationships rather than plundering your address book for short-term results.

10

The Zone System

This chapter helps you to:

- Take gradual, easy steps towards new conversations
- Practise and gain support before you put yourself into demanding contexts
- Gradually develop your skills at interaction and connecting
- Move closer to the kind of people who can make a difference

From comfort zone to infinity

You might dislike working to a plan, but a structure can help in many ways. You can experiment at your own speed, trying things out in relatively safe environments. By increasing risk and difficulty in increments you can tackle harder situations when you've some useful experience and feedback under your belt.

The Zone System is set out below (with grovelling apologies to the great Ansel Adams, whose Zone System for exposure is famous in silver-based photography). This Zone System is about people and connections. It's designed to provide a gradual, step-by-step approach so you can work your way through various people 'zones', starting easily and then progressing through six new levels of connection:

People Zones

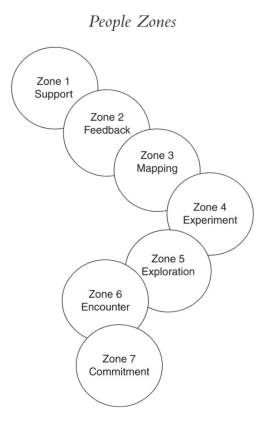

ZONE 1 – SUPPORT

ZONE 1 IS ABOUT GETTING ENCOURAGEMENT AND SUPPORT FROM PEOPLE YOU TRUST

Zone 1 is an important preparatory stage that most people ignore, preferring the high-risk strategy of throwing themselves into conversations they're not ready to handle. This Zone offers the gentlest form of outreach. Here you spend time with supportive people, talking with positive-minded friends about what you hope to achieve and what you think gets in the way.

Find two or three trusted contacts. With Zone 1 people you should feel able to pick up a phone without knowing exactly what to ask. Tell them what kind of help you need. Explain that you need to reach out to new people but you want to feel a little more confident about the process. Tell them you feel uncomfortable with networking and elevator pitches – they'll sympathize.

You're going to ask your Zone 1 contacts to do two important things: first, help you to remember your strengths and to think about why these might be helpful to others, and, second, help you to build confidence so that you can start talking about yourself without embarrassment.

Zone 1 contacts are:

- Easy to approach, and easy to talk to
- Naturally supportive, with positive ideas
- Capable of reminding you of your strengths and career highlights
- People who will encourage you to plan and make progress

Openings for a Zone 1 conversation:

- 'Can I ask for your help?'
- 'Have you got time for a coffee this week?'
- 'I could do with some advice.'

How do you know if you've done enough Zone 1 conversations?

- You have found a support team who will be there for you on the journey ahead
- The idea of talking about yourself seems less daunting
- You're starting to see that your experience may be of interest to other people
- Your confidence is improving and you feel ready to have a Zone 2 conversation

ZONE 2 – FEEDBACK

ZONE 2 IS ABOUT PRACTISING AND IMPROVING

After receiving encouragement you might feel ready to 'get out there'. Zone 2 offers the opportunity of a dummy run to test out ways of interacting in a safe space where getting it wrong won't be damaging.

You learn best from mistakes. Zone 2 is your chance to make them, adjust and improve. This zone isn't about impressing or influencing, or getting new contacts. It's not about emotional support – that's Zone 1. This zone gets you clear, objective feedback about how you project yourself.

Zone 2 contacts are:

- People who know what a confident performance sounds like and can give you honest but helpful feedback. They're naturally good at drawing out the best in you
- Capable of saying more than 'that sounds wrong' – choose people who can explain how you can improve, who will suggest phrases for you to try for yourself
- People you can go back to in the future even if you decide to change direction

Openings for a Zone 2 conversation:

- 'I need to start talking to people – can I practise on you first?'
- 'I'm wondering how I should approach new contacts – can I ask your advice?'

(*'Starter Script A – Testing Your Material' offers more questions.*)

How do you know if you've done enough Zone 2 conversations?

- You've practised small talk, open questions and follow-up questions (*see* Chapter 7)
- You've learned to ask questions so they are not complicated and don't sound intrusive or naive
- You've practised talking about yourself briefly and positively
- You're curious about where to try your new techniques out

ZONE 3 – MAPPING

ZONE 3 IS ABOUT ASKING PEOPLE YOU KNOW
WHERE TO BEGIN YOUR EXPLORATION

Zone 3 turns the spotlight off you and provides maps for where exploring might take you. The question 'where should I look?' is easy to ask, because you're talking to people you know well. It's also easy to answer. You're starting to build knowledge and pick up background detail. Soon you'll have a target list of interesting people you'd like to talk to – but you don't need to approach them just yet.

This may be a fairly quick process – one person can sometimes provide nearly everything you need. Zone 1 or 2 contacts can often recommend people to approach.

Zone 3 contacts are:

- Individuals who know about market trends, new entrants, who's up and who's down
- People with relevant (ideally recent) work experience and sector knowledge
- People who can point you towards specific organizations and people so your next steps are clear

Openings for a Zone 3 conversation:

- 'I'm trying to find people who work in XXX sector. Can I pick your brain?'
- 'I'm exploring at the moment and could do with some good ideas.'

(*'Starter Script B – Information Gathering' offers more questions.*)

Questions to ask in a Zone 3 conversation:

- 'I'm interested in sector X. What organizations should I be looking at?'
- 'Who are the biggest players?'
- 'What does cutting edge look like?'
- 'What are the interesting niche organizations?'
- 'Who knows everybody in this world?'
- 'I don't want to ring people cold. What do you recommend as my next step?'

WARM REFERRALS

Note the final bullet point. Don't ring people cold. Starting 'you don't know me' sets up suspicion and resistance. Always ask for a warm introduction, which means your contact rings or emails the next person in the chain, with a brief explanation about why you will be in touch. That way the contact you're approaching knows several important things: you're a genuine enquirer, you're not selling anything, and you're known to someone they trust. Getting beyond those three hurdles is often all it takes to persuade someone to see you.

How do you know if you've done enough Zone 3 conversations?

- You know where to begin to look
- You know what background research you need to do

- You've got some excellent questions for Zone 4
- You've got three or four warm introductions ready for Zone 5

ZONE 4 – EXPERIMENT

ZONE 4 IS ABOUT BEGINNING EXPLORATION BY REACHING OUT TO PEOPLE YOU ALREADY KNOW

Although Zone 3 has generated warm introductions to new contacts, keep those in your back pocket for the moment. Right now you're going to limit yourself to people you know, but this time with the aim of asking questions and talking about yourself.

Zone 4 is a controlled experiment taking you outside your comfort zone. Armed with encouragement and feedback on your communication style, you're good to go. But you don't want to fall flat on your face, so start by practising in a relatively safe context – with people you already know.

Think about contacts you know through work, study, family or social connections. Who might have relevant experience? Specific sector knowledge is helpful, but so are people who know people. Approach them openly asking for advice, indicating what you're hoping to achieve. (Warning: you may be tempted to approach very high level contacts at this stage. *See* Chapter 8 to understand why you save these high-value cards until later in the game.)

Zone 4 contacts are:

- People you feel relatively confident approaching
- People with particular insights into sectors or organizations
- People who will give you additional feedback on your messages to the marketplace
- People who can give you warm connections to Zone 5 contacts

Openings for a Zone 4 conversation:

- 'We haven't spoken for a while, but it would be great to meet up for a coffee.'
- 'I hope you don't mind me picking your brain.'
- 'I'm trying to find out a lot more about XXX and I know you're the right person to talk to.'
- 'I don't want to ring people cold. What do you recommend as my next step?'

(*'Starter Script C – Networking Appointments' offers more questions.*)

Dangers in Zone 4 conversations:

- Going in too early before you know what to say
- Asking for things that people can't deliver
- Avoiding face-to-face meetings with all their benefits (*see* Chapter 5)
- Demanding full access to your contact's little black book (we pass on contacts in small batches, never wholesale)

How do you know if you've done enough Zone 4 conversations?

- You have some good names and connections in your notebook, and all you need is the green light of an introduction
- You're ready to have a well-planned conversation with someone you don't yet know

ZONE 5 – EXPLORATION

ZONE 5 IS ABOUT REACHING OUT TO PEOPLE YOU'VE NEVER MET BEFORE

Zone 5 is the first step completely outside your comfort zone. These face-to-face conversations are like Zone 4, but this time with people you've never met before. If that idea bothers you and you think you'll be tongue-tied, you haven't spent enough time in Zones 1 and 2. However, don't postpone Zone 5 too long. Reaching new contacts gives exciting results.

From your Zone 3 results, draw up a list of target organizations – a starting list of 12–15 keeps things manageable. Spend time each week learning something new about each of your targets, trying to get closer to them through mutual connections. Seek out people who are in or near these organizations. Use LinkedIn to search for organization names and for people to speak to. If you're seeking sector information you'll be much more credible if you've done some background research.

Who do you want to talk to at Zone 5? *See* the Zone 4 list. Same types of people, but this time you're reaching out to people you've never met before. With warm introductions from your Zone 3 and 4 people, the reason why you're approaching them should already be clear.

Note: a very quick route to Zone 5 is available if you're part of any kind of alumni network. People joining such networks understand that occasionally they will receive requests for information and advice from other alumni. They are in a sense 'pre-contracted' – they've already agreed to help. You still have to approach them sensibly, asking things they'll be comfortable in delivering.

Zone 5 contacts are:

- People who have been introduced to you in Zone 1–4 conversations
- People with useful contacts
- People with interesting perspectives on the work they do
- People who really understand the sector they work in
- People who may make warm introductions for you

Ways to begin a Zone 5 conversation:

- 'I believe Alec mentioned that I might be in touch...?'
- 'I'd love to pick your brain, and I promise not to overstay my welcome. Would you be free next week some time?'
- 'Alec tells me that you're the go-to person in this field.'

Questions to ask in a Zone 5 conversation:

- 'Thanks for meeting me. If you remember from my email, I'm trying to talk to a range of people who know this sector inside out.'
- 'Who are the biggest players in this sector? Who's doing the most interesting projects?'
- 'This has been incredibly helpful – thank you so much. I'm just wondering ... who else do you think I should be having a conversation with? Really? Great suggestion. Listen, I hate ringing people cold – would you do me an enormous favour and make an introduction for me so he knows why I'll be calling?'

(Again, 'Starter Script C – Networking Appointments' offers further questions for Zones 4 and 5.)

Dangers in Zone 5 conversations:

- Trying to get a Zone 5 conversation without a warm introduction
- Trying to do everything by phone or email and neglecting the power of meeting in person
- Lack of prepared questions and practised small talk
- Operating on 'broadcast' rather than 'receive'. Believing you have to push or sell

How do you know if you've done enough Zone 5 conversations?

Sometimes you may feel you've found all you need, but in broad terms you can continue having Zone 5 conversations forever, keeping you up to date and connected with interesting people

By practising Zone 5 conversations it means you'll be ready for unplanned meetings – Zone 6

ZONE 6 – ENCOUNTER

ZONE 6 IS ABOUT UNPLANNED MEETINGS WITH NEW PEOPLE

Zone 6 is where you encounter someone randomly. Of course, 'randomly' is slightly disingenuous. You might, for example, go to an event with the aim of talking to certain kinds of people, or one specific individual. You don't know if you'll have to introduce yourself or if someone will do it for you. You're not entirely sure how it will happen, but you want to be ready.

Sometimes you'll have to actively engineer encounters. When you're at an event, asking smart questions will often lead naturally to introductions to others in the room with relevant experience – it's a context where warm introductions are easy. If there's someone present you'd really like to meet, ask someone who knows this person to walk you over so you can say hello (often the event host will be happy to do this).

Readiness prepares you for genuinely random meetings – on a train journey, for example. Or bumping into someone who arrives at a building the same time as you do. Or a great contact you happen to meet at a child's birthday party. A few well-prepared techniques for engaging people in conversation helps in multiple situations.

Zone 6 encounters may be fairly brief. Once you've found interests in common, ask for and offer a business card. Make notes on the reverse to remember what you talked about so you can reach out within the next 2–3 days by email, phone, or by inviting someone to connect on LinkedIn.

Zone 6 contacts are:

- People you choose to run into at live events
- People you meet in an unplanned or chance way
- Potential Zone 3, 5 or 7 contacts. In other words, they may help you map, they may help you explore or they may get you close to a decision. You just don't know until you ask
- People who will make warm introductions for you

Questions to ask in a Zone 6 conversation:

- 'How are you enjoying this event?'
- 'What brings you here today?'

(See also 'Starter Script D – Networking Encounters'. You can find more on encounter-focused questions in Chapter 7).

Dangers in Zone 6 conversations:

- Failing to sound relaxed and natural
- Dominating the conversation and crowding personal space
- Sounding as if you're more interested in what you say than its impact (*see* Chapter 2)
- Talking too much and not demonstrating good listening skills (*see* Chapter 6)
- Talking about yourself without finding your authentic voice (*see* Chapter 7)

- See the Zone 5 list – most apply here – especially where you make the conversation feel transactional, dull or pushy

How do you know if you've done enough Zone 6 conversations?

- Again, 'enough' is probably a false notion. Unless you never leave home, you'll always have these encounters
- Many Zone 6 conversations can become Zone 7 conversations if you move them in the right direction
- You acquire key information – plus confidence in handling conversations and reaching out to strangers
- You're ready for a Zone 7 conversation

ZONE 7 – COMMITMENT

ZONE 7 IS ABOUT GETTING IN FRONT OF PEOPLE WHO CAN COMMIT TO ACTION

Zone 7 is where you're talking to decision-makers who will forward your agenda: this might be about hiring your services, investing in you, appointing you, buying from you. It might be about recommending you to other senior colleagues and budget controllers. It could be a low-level commitment like inviting you to work as an intern, or a high-level commitment like promoting you or creating a job around you.

Zone 7 puts you in front of people who can make a difference to your future, your income and your reputation. You're practised and confident enough. You know how to build a conversation, listen hard and how to talk about your strengths. By now your communication skills are honed to the point when you can match what you do to organizational needs.

If you can't find someone who can make a high level connection for you, then you might try a speculative approach. This is of course stone cold compared to the strategies for person-hopping recommended in previous zones, but it might be your only option. Have you really exhausted the possibilities on offer from existing contacts? Try emailing about 20 trusted contacts and asking the question 'Do you know anyone who knows Ben Smith of XYZ Holdings' – this may quickly take you past first base.

Zone 7 contacts are:

- People capable of signing off on a contract or budget or a new role
- People with contacts who have the same power
- People whose recommendations will really count and create shortcuts

Questions to ask in a Zone 7 conversation:

- 'What do you need?'
- 'What's your biggest headache?' 'What gets in the way of success for you?'
- 'What solutions have you already tried?'
- 'I've worked on something like this before – can I tell you about it?'

Checklist – Are you ready for Zone 7 conversations?

- Do you know enough about the organization you're talking to? Detailed homework is vital
- Can you talk about yourself convincingly? Can you present evidence which makes someone feel you're worth spending money on?
- Can you talk about your strengths without sounding embarrassed or over the top?
- Do you have snappy short stories evidencing your abilities?
- Do you have a clear reason for wanting the conversation (you know the organization's problems and you can show how you are part of the solution)?

Dangers in Zone 7 conversations:

- You avoid them forever because you never feel confident enough to take them, even when you have a perfect introduction. Don't set the bar so high that you never get to Zone 7
- You really are underprepared, because you skipped Zones 1 and 2. Remove hesitation and 'I can't do this' thinking out of your system before you put yourself in front of important people

How do you know if you've done enough Zone 7 conversations?

- You've achieved a specific objective, for example you've secured funding, identified a mentor, won a contract, got your promotion
- You might keep on setting up Zone 7 conversations, moving by recommendation from one decision-maker to another
- Move back through the Zones again when you need to. Where you dip back in depends on your confidence level and whether you need new connections

Taking things to the next zone

Keep on asking people for information, ideas and connections. When you find Zone 1 conversations easy, take the next step. Go back to your Zone 2 or 3 contacts and say 'remember you offered to introduce me to Dave Smith...? If you could do that now, that would be brilliant'.

The Zone System underlines the way that people will happily pave the way for you. Don't risk a broken connection by approaching people cold or not knowing what to say if you encounter someone by chance. And remember that your best way of getting a meeting is always going to be through the intervention of someone you already know. The great thing about this method is no one asks 'Why are you here?'. Your connection has already made that clear.

How the Zone System can help you

- It enables you to begin networking even if you feel you don't know anyone
- You can start small and easy in low-risk situations
- You learn to open ask for help without feeling you're exploiting people
- You practise asking interesting questions which don't sound pushy or naive
- You get used to talking about yourself and what interests you
- You develop authentic ways of talking about what you have to offer
- You will receive encouragement, feedback, support and new connections
- You will rarely, if ever, ring anyone cold

11

Projecting yourself on paper and online

This chapter helps you to:

- Think about when it's appropriate to put something in writing
- Watch out for problems of tone
- Learn to condense and pitch short outlines
- Avoid classic errors in written communication
- Tell rather than sell

When you're not in the room...

Sometimes your best chance to influence is by using the written word. This may be straightforward – for example when providing simple instructions. Often the task is more complex – when you're trying to motivate or persuade, or asking someone to do something difficult. Even giving praise or saying thank you requires careful attention to tone. When you read something that leaves you feeling irritated or slightly offended, you might choose not to respond.

Written communication is a vital influencing tool. It can make people feel warm and well disposed towards you. It can persuade people to step outside their comfort zone and help you. On the other hand it can close down a relationship. A good writing style takes practice but looks effortless. As Somerset Maugham wrote: 'The best style is the one you don't notice.' Writing to influence depends on brevity, tone and impact.

Chapter 14 outlines the way people try to use one document – a CV – to gain traction. A CV (or a letter, or an email out of the blue) is a weak door opener. If someone meets you and finds you interesting they'll ask for a CV or look you up online, but a document should never be your first or preferred strategy. People, and conversations, open doors. Written communication can create leverage, but you should always be looking for a chance to speak to someone.

Sometimes you can only present yourself in writing. Perhaps you can't get in the room with someone but want your message to get through. You may know the recipient well ('summarize those ideas for me in an email') or you could be pitching to a stranger. You might be setting out your stall (a job application or appraisal).

Getting your story across

At events, people stick a CV under my nose and ask me for feedback. I place the offered CV face down, then ask 'What would you like a future employer to know about you? What makes you stand out?'. After some prompting, nearly everyone has an answer – which encourages me to believe that all of us can learn to communicate the best parts of ourselves. People talk about what they do well, what they find exciting, about their background and their story. I listen, then I turn the CV face up, and read to see if any of this rich material appears in the first five lines of text. It rarely does.

The most important editing job you do is this: ask yourself 'What does my reader need to know about?' This applies to a LinkedIn page just as much as a CV. Make sure the most important points play out while you hold the reader's attention – items worth highlighting include skills, know-how, unusual experience – anything that differentiates and prevents you being ordinary, 'vanilla', invisible.

It's common to read a CV or LinkedIn profile and then meet a very different person; capturing yourself accurately in writing is harder than it looks. Exaggeration is commonplace, but equally often people under-explain or fail to mention the breadth of their experience. They justify this saying 'they'll understand me better when they met me' – but if your document doesn't get you through the door, that's not going to happen.

Another common mistake is trying to make your writing deliver things which are hard or even impossible. Trying to persuade, convince, flatter, mollify or motivate through written text is possible, but it takes distinct skill. Even explaining your strong points takes practice – which is why so many people fill their LinkedIn profile with clichés ('self-starting', 'highly motivated', 'a team player who can work alone').

Putting yourself in the right box

Projecting yourself in writing isn't about writing forcefully. It's about understanding that most readers are busy and impatient. They want to extract information in the shortest possible time.

Many dislike being pushed into a category. For example, you may occasionally chair meetings but you may resent being described as a 'committee person'. You probably want people to think of you outside the terms of your job title. However, when you want people to understand essential messages quickly, instant labels can be useful. Sometimes the box you're pushed into is a poor fit. 'Positive pigeon-holing' means that the shorthand label applied to you is accurate. For example, you might want people to know that you're an experienced engineer with unusually strong people skills. If so, make that your first message rather than extensively listing your qualifications, experience and various job titles. A quick overview helps people to understand you quickly (*see* Summary Statements in Chapter 3).

Your electronic shop window

If someone wants to know more about you, the quickest route to discovery is a computer keyboard. Only a short while ago people were advised that they 'might like to think about' their online presence. Now it's vital. Some commentators estimate that around 80 per cent of recruiters 'Google' potential candidates. Research by ExecuNet showed that 35 per cent of recruiters admitted they eliminated a candidate because of what they found online. The same survey showed that only a third of candidates searched the Internet for information about themselves.

In the past most professionals relied on personal websites to project their reputation. Now LinkedIn provides the most obvious form of online CV. If it works, it works effortlessly – a simple summary of what you do well. If it doesn't, it sends out a very different message. Try this. Search LinkedIn for people you have worked with in the past. Soon you will find at least one person you can't find at all. Your immediate assumptions might be that someone is retired, out of the game, or feels too special to be listed. You feel something similar when you find a page containing no photograph and only bare or out-of-date information – this easily suggests that someone doesn't know how or doesn't care.

'LinkedIn is still where the majority of UK-based business contacts and recruiters congregate, so it remains a 'must be' place online. Before you start engaging with others on LinkedIn, spend time to develop a comprehensive and visually appealing profile so you make a strong first impression. Write a headline that means something to those in your field of work and that includes relevant keywords (not just the job title), upload a professional headshot, write a summary that shows your abilities and expertise, fill in your past positions and ensure your career data matches the information and dates on your CV, as hiring managers will check for consistency straight away. To really stand out, enrich your profile with strong images, for instance an appropriate header photo, a link to your presentations that are in the public domain. Upload any videos that your organization might have, find links to articles you have written or images of your accreditations. Sharing sound information about yourself on LinkedIn is the bare minimum. Making your profile visually appealing shows that you know what matters in a digital world.'

Ruth Winden, social media expert & career coach

Think about who will be looking you up. If you're in a job but looking for a new one, take care not to upset your current employer by going public about your plans to move on. On LinkedIn it's equally unwise to overemphasize the fact that you're between jobs (*see* Chapter 14).

Value micro-messages

Where data is in oversupply, we value it more when it comes in small packages. Rather than complete courses or business books, many customers of Harvard Business Publishing buy single-chapter extracts and slide decks, sometimes very late at night when they are preparing for the next day.

When we need to commit to writing, we often over-deliver. Applicants for grants or a place on a course of study commonly write far more than is needed. Oversupply means the reader has to work harder to extract relevant meaning. Today's pace of life means few people have the patience to do so.

Let's imagine you've met someone interesting yesterday at a business event and you've agreed to follow up by email. What are you going to write? Without thinking you might send your CV. That's a big ask (*see* Chapter 8) – a time-consuming and potentially complex task that your contact will probably wish to delay. So you might decide to send an email giving an overview of your work history, your skills, and a list of the services you could offer. Slow down. All that information? Really?

Rethink your approach. Forget what you're itching to say, but ask yourself 'What does this person *need to know in order to commit to the next step?*' Be clear about what that next step is – another introduction, some information, a meeting? Bullet points ensure brevity and increase the chances that someone will act. For example:

Hi Jo

It was great to bump into you today. As promised, here's something about my background and interests:

- Experience of customer communications in a range of sectors including design, home furnishings, sporting goods
- Worked in New York, London, Frankfurt. Fluent in German and English
- In my most recent role achieved measurably improved customer satisfaction scores through a focus on the retail experience
- Currently exploring how this professional experience can be applied to customer interaction in the online gaming sector

It would be great to meet up in town next week if you're free – I could do Wednesday or Thursday.
Many thanks
Rob

The above sample email isn't designed to win a literary prize. It's brief, crisp, gets straight to the point, captures just four important messages, and has a polite and not too pushy call to action. It starts informally but doesn't take liberties with tone. It can be read in about 35 seconds (time it!). It makes an immediate response relatively painless. Try this approach next time you want to reach out to someone after meeting them – make it easy for someone to take the conversation to the next level.

Questions to ask yourself before you write and send

- It is going to the right person?
- What do I want the reader to understand, believe and above all do as a result of my communication?
- What exactly do I need to say to have this effect on the reader?
- What is the most appropriate medium – speech, face to face, telephone or writing – for getting my message received and understood by the recipient?
- What is going to hinder good communication?
- What feedback should I expect in order to tell me I have communicated effectively?

Reader pain levels

Clear, plain English is relatively rare – writers today often overcompress by using textspeak (even in emails) – for example 'responses ASAP', which can come across as very pushy. Just as often we overcomplicate, hiding a simple request within a long paragraph. Complicated text can also conceal what we want to say – how many times have you read an email and had to ask yourself what it wants you to do?

Be clear of the outcome of any document. With a business report, for example, what you write at first is your way of thinking around the topic. When you re-draft you'll often find that this opening can be trimmed, or cut.

Considerable research has been undertaken about how we read, looking at the high-speed way we draw out relevant information. Analysts focus not just on reader preferences but reader discomfort. Some readers describe something akin to physical irritation when forced to read text that is compressed into tight, indigestible blocks. It's interesting in an age of text-speak how often we use paragraphs – blocks of text – when bullet points are clearer.

Classic errors in presenting yourself in writing

- Your goal is unclear. Think about what you want to happen after your document has been read
- Saying too much. Writing everything down in the hope that something sticks
- Saying too little. Brevity is admirable, but sometimes you need to explain or persuade before pushing for a response
- Style frustrates more than it communicates. This could be because sentences are too long and unclear, or you frustrate the reader with bad grammar, words used incorrectly, or poor punctuation.
- Inappropriate tone. Careful attention to tone makes the difference between gentle persuasion and sounding petulant or demanding
- Lack of clarity. If someone needs to read your writing more than once, it's not communicating the desired message
- Ambiguity. What you say can be interpreted in a number of ways and you may appear to be saying the opposite of what you intend

- Multiple purposes. Send a short email on one topic rather than a long document covering a range of subjects
- Writing as though it's an academic dissertation. Many people switch to an overstiff, formal style when writing
- Writing that doesn't achieve its intended outcome. You may believe you are asking somebody for a favour, but your email may sound as though you are taking liberties
- Text that misrepresents your real personality. In an effort to sound friendly you may come across as naive or pushy. Attempting to be firm you may come across as rude
- Failing to use plain English, for example 'utilize' instead of 'use', 'terminate' rather than 'end'
- Using 'insider language' or jargon. If the reader doesn't understand it, he or she may feel excluded and possibly stupid
- Peppering your document with clichés or the empty language that plagues the modern workplace such as 'paradigm shift', 'thinking outside the box', 'deliverables' or 'gaining traction'.
- Lack of insight into the context – sometimes described as understanding the hidden agenda. For example, pestering someone who you know receives 200-300 similar messages every day, or making niggling criticisms when someone is working under immense pressure
- Not reading it out loud before you consider it finished. If it sounds wrong, it almost certainly is wrong

When formality gets in the way

When writing, it's easy to think that 'important' means 'formal'. You sense that the document matters, so your mind remembers a time when you had to write with great care – writing essays and sitting examinations. Therefore you feel it's appropriate to use longer sentences and fancier language. You find yourself writing: 'I would appreciate the opportunity of a more detailed discussion at some date in the future' rather than 'I hope we can meet soon'; or 'give consideration to' rather than 'think about'. You use several words when one will do ('in the great majority of cases' instead of 'usually' or 'at this moment in time' rather than 'now').

Follow the advice of Winston Churchill who recommended single-syllable words which hail from our Anglo-Saxon past: '*the short words are the best, and the old words best of all*'.

Adults sometimes used complex constructions to show their level of education, so they say 'Our current requirement is for...' rather than 'We need...'. We are all tempted to use long words to show off, but short ones have more punch. So you might 'list core competencies', but colleagues would probably rather you talked about what you can do. Short words have impact – a fact well known to advertising copywriters (for example 'loves the jobs you hate') and public speakers ('I have a dream'). Plain English works: it is absorbed quicker, puts fewer people off, and helps you say what you mean.

Accuracy

It's an inescapable fact: spelling, grammar and punctuation matter. They matter because what you write is taken as a reflection of how you work. A failure to check detail and quality in an email is likely to be seen as an indication that you make mistakes everywhere. Basic errors in your writing often mean your message is rejected from the outset.

Get it right. If you can't do it yourself, find someone who can; even proficient writers aren't always the best proofreaders. If your document matters, put it under the nose of someone with an almost painful attention to detail (but don't let them make your language more stuffy). You can't rely on your computer's spellchecker – it can't tell the difference between two correctly spelled words (e.g. 'too' and 'two', 'their' and 'there') and it won't catch simple word confusions, e.g. 'bought' and 'brought'. It's worth learning about common word confusions (disinterested/uninterested, lose/loose and refute/deny) and words that sound similar (homophones) such as stationery/stationary, effect/affect and compliment/complement.

Most people reading your material are at least mildly sceptical. They're used to people and organizations who overpromise and underdeliver. They are highly unlikely to accept at face value any claims you make about your own ability unless they're backed up with objective evidence – for example, positive references on LinkedIn often carry more weight than bald assertions of your strengths.

Tone, and saying difficult things

If a document is important, think hard about the one or two things it really needs to say. Write them down as bullet points, then wrap them up with as little padding as possible. When you've finished, don't press 'send' if the deadline isn't immediate. Let an email sit for a while in your outbox and you'll often realize that you've missed out an important point, or you'll discover an error. You may want to rethink completely.

'The time to begin writing an article is when you have finished it to your satisfaction. By that time you begin to clearly and logically perceive what it is you want to say.'

Mark Twain, US author

If it's a really difficult message, ask yourself if it should be delivered in writing at all. If you must send it this way, then leaving something in draft for 24 hours often provides a good chance to reflect – and check you've adopted the right tone. It should go without saying that you shouldn't finalize any important document if you're feeling tired or bad-tempered.

If you've got something difficult to say, avoid putting it in writing. For example, challenging someone's behaviour in the workplace is generally much easier to do face to face – exact words can be forgotten and you can give full concentration to getting the tone right. Asking for a favour or giving a complement is generally also much better done in the room. There are of course times where you have to commit something to the page because the wording matters and needs to be kept on file – for example in a written reference or warning.

Tone is hardest to manage when you really, really want a result; it's easy to sound too eager or slightly desperate. You might ask for too much too soon (perhaps saying 'I'll call you next week' where it's more appropriate to say 'How about if I call you next week?').

Saying what needs saying rather than pushing

When writing fails to work it's often because we're unclear about intended outcomes. An approach that is essentially 'I'll say lots of things about what I can do and see what they find interesting' usually leads to vagueness. The American academic and marketing specialist Flint McGlaughlin is widely quoted: 'clarity trumps persuasion'.

'The average person is assaulted with a barrage of 577 new marketing messages per week. If we could somehow wire the mind of the consumer as they sift through the conundrum of emails, snail mails, banners and commercials... we would probably hear a resounding response: "I don't have time to listen, and I don't believe you anyway".'

Flint McGlaughlin, How To Earn The Trust
Of A Sceptical Consumer

Spend more time thinking about what you want to say rather than worrying about pushing the reader's 'buy' button. If someone can't see and hear you being tongue in cheek, statements about your talents may sound overblown. Having said that, don't be afraid to express enthusiasm – written language can convey energy and curiosity just as effectively as the things you've learned to say in person.

Top 10 messages from this chapter

1 Don't write if you can phone. Don't phone if you can see someone face to face.

2 If you're trying to say something difficult, avoid putting it in writing.

3 Understand that an email, a letter, a CV or a brochure is more likely to confirm a decision than prompt one. Relationships, not documents, set things in motion.

4 Reduce reader pain levels and make it easier for the recipient to do what you want them to do.

5 Use bullet points to break up long passages of text into easily digested sound bites.

6 Do everything in your power to communicate accurately without errors, which suggest sloppy attention to detail.

7 Be cautious when it comes to tone, especially if you're trying to be chatty, funny or pushy – if it feels uncomfortable then it will probably be read that way.

8 Practise writing shorter sentences that use shorter words. Avoid complexity, jargon or anything that could give the reader a problem.

9 Be clear about the outcomes you seek. Don't ask for too much.

10 Don't be tempted to write down everything you think of. Write the smallest amount of information that your reader needs to see in order to commit to the next step.

12

Easier, more impactful, presentations

This chapter helps you to:

- Take nervousness seriously, but don't let it get in the way of great preparation
- Put yourself in the shoes of the average audience member
- See how a great talk is all about opening, closing and good links
- Avoid classic errors that lose audience attention
- Identify presentation techniques that set you apart from the crowd

The white knuckle ride of public speaking

Even smart people don't prepare enough before high visibility events. People who hate public speaking talk about preparation but never quite do it. Their real plan is: 'I'll make it up when I get there.' The most likely reason is that you need to visualize what an event will feel like — and that can provoke anxiety. Because we'd rather not face up to fear, we rationalize inadequate forms of preparation.

One of the reasons presentations and talks matter is that they enhance your visibility. Whether you're hoping for a promotion or wanting to be noticed outside your organization, speaking in public is a kind of screen test. If someone senior or influential is in the audience, it matters: it's an audition for a bigger role, an interesting project. Because confidence, communication skills and self-projection are important in so many areas of working life your ability to stand up and speak is often taken (quite inaccurately in many cases) as an indication of competence in a hundred other areas.

When coaching clients for important presentations, I ask them to pretend that I'm an audience member. However, they usually start 'when I get there I will talk about…'. I need to know the *exact* words they will begin with. So if your plan is 'I'll probably begin by talking about quality and added value…' that means you have no plan at all. You need to know the precise words you will use to start and end the presentation – and how you will link sections.

Beginning with the end in mind

Think about *why* you're going to speak. Someone has invited you to inform, to fill a gap, to provide variety, to lift the audience after a heavy session. Some organizers will ask you to list learning objectives in advance. This is helpful because it requires you to complete the sentence 'At the end of my presentation people will…'. Ask the organizers what they want in terms of style as well as content. Ask about the time slot for your talk. A 50-minute slot often works very well. It's hard to keep an audience's attention for longer than about 40 minutes, unless you can break things up with exercises and group discussions, A 50-minute slot allows for the previous session to overrun slightly, 40 minutes where you talk, then 5-10 minutes for questions at the end. Don't overrun – speakers who finish late are often not invited back.

'What do you want your audience to DO when you've finished speaking? Write down exactly the action you'd like them to take in an ideal world. This statement, or an iteration of it, will form the last words you say.'

Richard Tierney, author of The Introverted Presenter

Visualize likely members of your audience. Think about what they would find useful. Imagine what they are expecting. Remember all the dull speeches you have sat through – and do better. Think about good talks you can still remember – the speaker probably used humour, storytelling and analogy. Don't underestimate the importance of being entertaining – which isn't about telling jokes (although well-pitched humour can win an audience over), but about concise enthusiasm. Audiences enjoy listening to people who know their stuff and speak with energy about the things that matter to them.

When you finish speaking, someone will make a beeline for you to tell you how helpful your talk was – this may surprise you as this person might have looked uninterested. Think of that response the next time you warm up before giving a talk. Don't worry about being a great speaker, just imagine how you will help one special individual go home feeling informed and inspired. Talk as if you're addressing just one person and the whole audience will feel that you are speaking directly and intimately to each of them.

Six stages to smarter preparation

Stage 1 – Before you draft your talk

- Before you write anything down, think about why you have been asked to speak. If you were in the audience, what would you hope to hear?
- If there are several speakers, watch out for overlap. Compare ideas with other speakers at the planning stage to avoid repetition
- Write down the main message – ideally in one sentence – you're going to get across. For example: 'I want my audience to understand that you don't have to be an extrovert to communicate well and

make new connections.' Now you know what your talk is about. Your next job is to make sure your audience goes home understanding the message

- Think about three or four subsidiary points you need to make. Again, images might help you to clarify what you want to say, and later on will help you remember
- Now your speech has a route map. Don't overcomplicate things further or distract yourself from your planned direction

Stage 2 – Drafting

- Write down the last three sentences of your talk. What will your final, summarizing phrase be? How will you close?
- Decide on the steps your speech needs to take to get to this conclusion. If you get to more than six steps, it's probably too complicated
- What stories can you tell? Are they easy to follow? Short enough?
- Can you think of a good, fresh, metaphor or analogy to get your point across?
- People write speeches in the same way they write reports, but you don't speak the same way you write. Improvise directly into a recording device (your mobile phone will probably work for this). Don't worry if you repeat yourself or stumble – just keep talking. Play it back and write down the phrases that have impact. Repeat until you've got some strong phrases. This is 'talking onto paper', capturing the freshness of spontaneous speech
- Now write the first draft of your speech. Keep sentences short. Use dashes – like this – to break up

text, rather than normal punctuation. Some speakers use only bullet points or lines set out like a poem

- Mark where you plan to emphasize or pause
- Make your word count fit your timeslot. Richard Tierney advises: 'Public speaking normally runs at three words every two seconds, or about 90 words a minute.' Therefore, a 600-word speech will take between six and seven minutes, depending on pauses
- Work hard on phrases that link the various sections of your talk. They are often the weakest parts of presentations
- Now write the opening three sentences. An audience decides within 30 seconds whether you're worth its attention. Communicate authority and show that you're not going to be boring. You don't need a joke or a snappy sound bite, just certainty and clarity: 'I'm delighted to be here today. I want to talk to you about how every person in this room can be a successful networker.'

Stage 3 – Visuals

- Would a visual image convey an idea better than words? How about a physical prop?
- Don't be afraid of using PowerPoint®. Used well, it maintains audience attention. Three or four bullet points per slide – plus one image – works well
- Make bullet points tempt, tease or encapsulate – 'work the magic' demands attention more than 'make sure you maintain your audience's attention throughout'. People listen more intently when they need to unpack something

- Slides shouldn't overexplain, but present a puzzle – your audience eagerly awaits the solution
- The worst presentations contain complicated diagrams and extensive text that the presenter then reads off the screen. Less is much, much more.

Stage 4 – The day before

- Learn the opening three sentences and the last three sentences. When you speak don't deviate from what you have learned. As you become more confident you will memorize longer sections of your talks, especially links
- Try to get a good night's sleep. Read your talk through twice before you go to sleep (it helps your unconscious brain mull it over while you sleep, and also helps you remember parts of it without really trying). Don't worry about memorizing too much at this stage, and do not be tempted to make further changes
- Wear clothes that are smart enough to convey authority but comfortable enough not to distract you

Stage 5 – At the venue

- Give yourself plenty of time to get to the event. Sitting in on an earlier talk helps you pick up the vibe and get to know the audience. Ask how the event is going and what topics have already gone down well
- Get to the venue early so you can walk around in the space where you will be speaking. Get used to standing in position and see where movement is possible. Watch out for trip hazards, particularly loose cables. If you're on a stage, note carefully where the stage ends so you don't fall off it!

- Find out who will be introducing you – consider handing over a very short printed biography so you know exactly what will be said. Find out who will manage questions
- Handouts should be close at hand; check who will help you to distribute them
- If you're using PowerPoint, check that everything works and ensure that a new computer hasn't reformatted your slides. Make sure you know how to advance images faultlessly

Stage 6 – When you're on your feet

- Walk on with your back straight, looking at the audience. Pause for a few seconds, then speak without looking at your notes. Do that and you're halfway to a great presentation
- To increase confidence and audience impact, stand with your feet slightly apart – as if you were on the gently rolling deck of a ship
- Don't shuffle papers. Don't take anything with you that you don't need
- Use the word 'you' frequently. When you do so, look at one member of your audience, keeping eye contact for a couple of seconds. Audiences respond better if they feel that the speech is directed at them personally
- Stand still unless you choose to move for effect. Don't wave your hands about – use them to consciously reinforce what you are saying
- Learn how to control your voice and extend its power. Research studies indicate that student audiences believe lecturers are more personable, knowledgeable and better organized simply as a result of voice training. Pausing helps people absorb what

you are saying and adds gravitas, and so does speaking
in a deeper pitch

- DO NOT be tempted to rethink or rewrite your
speech while you are giving it. If you are short of
time, know what material you can cut. Otherwise,
assume that the plan is good enough, and stick to it.

Structure

Old-school advice about public speaking says: tell them what
you're going to tell them, tell them, and then tell them what
you've told them. You might have reservations about this
approach. First, you bore people by telling them the same
thing three times. Also, you take away a powerful element in
communication – surprise. If you're watching a film you feel
robbed if a plot twist is given away in the trailer. Retain one
great idea for the last five minutes of your talk. The big advantage of the 'tell them three times' school is that it offers structure and clarity, but you can achieve that in better ways. For
example, mimic the way TV news programmes trail highlights
at the beginning and open them up in detail later. You might
start with a question: 'Have you ever wondered why some people look uncomfortable when you ask them what they do for
a living? More of that in a moment. Meanwhile...' Revealing
enthusiasm for your subject also draws people in: 'I'm fascinated as to why some teams work brilliantly and others fail,
and I want to share some of my discoveries with you.' Notice
the intimacy of that statement, starting with 'I' and ending with
'you'. Notice the informal easy language. Your primary task is
to engage your audience. This makes them better listeners but
also helps them remember you.

Plan your delivery speed, not cramming in too much – leave
them wanting more. Speaking too quickly and indistinctly

conveys anxiety. Slow down for emphasis, but speaking very slowly bores an audience and makes them think you're a slow thinker. Vary your speed, but keep things moving.

'Keep a calm, conversational pace. Imagine talking to one person and giving them time to take in what you have said before you move on to the next idea.'

Caroline Goyder, author of Gravitas

Run the right kind of movie

There's a theory in sports science that visualizing an action imprints itself on your brain as powerfully as an actual memory. Athletes are therefore encouraged to work hard at imagining how it feels to clear the bar or beat their previously best time.

Picture yourself finishing your talk with the audience fully on your side. Visualize details: how you will be standing, how your voice sounds, the speed and volume of your words, your eye contact with the audience. When that picture is strong and clear, run it repeatedly. Give yourself a visual reminder (such as a gold star on your notes) that will keep you connected to that internal movie.

Reading from a script or notes

One thing convinces an audience you're a novice – getting lost in your notes. The problem starts if your script works on the page and not as a talk (*see above*). Newcomers to public speaking report how it feels suddenly impossible to stand still, talk, think ahead and read at the same time. Their brain becomes so overloaded that they're unable to read their notes. This is why people get lost, miss out important sections or fail to see their next line.

Abandoning your notes may push your stress levels way into the red. Some speakers hold to the gold-standard of script-free presentation, others say that there are times when carefully crafted words matter, and it's easier to pitch them sensitively when they are pre-scripted. The main thing is to understand that speaking notes are an aid to your performance, not the basis of it.

'Cook the speech down to bullet points and examples, and then practise and practise until you can tell it like a story after dinner.'

Caroline Goyder

Try using pictures rather than notes. Professional storytellers often rely on a set of cartoon-like images as prompts, knowing that it's easier to flash-read an image than to absorb text. Try it – write out your script like the page of a comic, using cartoons and as few words as possible. Alternatively, use a strong image on each PowerPoint slide, print your slides in handout form, six slides to a page, and use that as a memory jogger.

You can deliver a lively, word-for-word presentation from a printed script – but it's not a simple matter of reading out loud. Write the way you speak, and rehearse. Experienced speakers make a scripted talk sound almost entirely impromptu. They look at their audience more often than they read, and they know the text well enough to deliver large chunks of it without looking down at all. Once you've got a few talks under your belt, memorize as much as you can. For a speech of up to 10 minutes, try learning all of it – few things impress an audience more than a speaker working without notes.

Don't misread silence

Don't be put off if an audience doesn't seem to respond. In big audiences people feel invisible, so more inclined to respond warmly. It's much easier to get a big audience to laugh or ask questions. Smaller audiences are always more reticent because each person feels exposed. This is even more evident when your small audience is naturally quiet. My wife Jan Dean taught creative writing workshops to Swedish school teachers, and each group reacted the same way – blank, unsmiling faces. Yet at the end of every annual session a small delegation would approach and tell Jan the workshop was the best they had ever attended.

Quiet audiences will always present a challenge. It's as though people deliberately choose not to signal that they're finding your material valuable and enjoyable. Trust anything that looks like a positive sign, such as intent listening, note taking or sustained eye contact. If you're not getting much back, don't be tempted to speed up or cut material – stick to your plan, but seek objective feedback afterwards. You can use the same material with two different audiences and get two differing reactions.

Stop apologizing

Nervous speakers apologize every few minutes. They say they were asked to speak at short notice. They apologize for having slides they haven't time to show you, for arriving late or having to leave early. They apologize for not providing enough handouts. This is approval-seeking behaviour, and signals that you're going to be difficult to listen to. People start looking at their watches or phones.

If something has seriously gone wrong, tell the audience what you are going to do to resolve the problem. Laptops and projectors fail on occasion and handouts get lost. Audiences want reassurance that this isn't going to detract from the experience. So, 'OK, we have no power so this morning instead of sitting through my slides you're going to hear some interesting stories'. Instead of 'I'm sorry that the handouts are badly

printed' go for 'Don't strain your eyes. I'll send you all an electronic copy first thing tomorrow'.

Avoid paperwork

Too many speakers plan to hold an audience's attention – and
then prevent them from listening by giving out documents
at the beginning. They feel it adds value or makes them look
more professional, but what happens is that you ask an audience
to divide its attention. Telling people that background documents are available later is usually enough for them to trust
their ears rather than their eyes. If you feel a handout is necessary to explain something, find a better way of communicating:
a story, an image, a diagram – show it on screen and keep it as
simple as possible.

Since most handouts are given only passing attention, make
them available at the end of your speech – after questions.
Leave business cards or fliers next to the pile of handouts.
Alternatively, put your email address on screen and commit
to sending out background documents and copies of slides on
request.

Don't automatically allow paper copies of your slides to be
given out at the same time that you speak. The danger is that
audiences stop listening and read the slides you'll be showing later. This is sometimes controversial – some organizers
believe that paper copies of PowerPoint presentations are
good for note-taking, and some participants find that seeing
slides on paper suits their learning style. Nevertheless, you
can be assured that your best chance of getting an audience's
attention is if they are just listening to you and doing nothing else.

If you have to provide paper copies of your slides, use
two strategies. First, use mainly visual images and only short,

teasing bullet points. That way, audiences stop trying to guess what you will say and listen carefully to decode what's on screen. The second strategy is to explicitly invite people not to read ahead because the slides are only a starting point. If people want more from you afterwards – handouts, slides, book recommendations – that's a great way of starting a whole new conversation.

Top 10 messages from this chapter

1 Most preparation fails to visualize the actual event.
2 Audiences have a deep-seated hunger to be entertained as well as informed.
3 Don't rush into writing a speech. Decide what you want it to say.
4 Plan the closing moments first. What message do you want to leave in the room?
5 Speak your words onto paper rather than starting with a written text and trying to shape it into a verbal presentation.
6 Plan and learn your opening three sentences with great care. Pay special attention to the links between the sections of your talk.
7 Don't overcomplicate or overdeliver. A few good points made well, with illustrations, stick in memory far longer than something long and complex.
8 Don't apologize, get lost in your text, speak inaudibly or run out of time like average presenters.
9 Use PowerPoint® for images and short bullet points that prompt curiosity.
10 Visualize yourself giving a well-received talk. Practise carefully enough to make sure it happens.

13

Managing the way your boss and others see you at work

This chapter helps you to:

- Understand how your reputation is shaped by key influencers at work
- Build an image aligned to the things your organization values
- Increase your visibility, particularly to decision-makers
- Enhance your career by thinking about how your boss sees you
- Avoid 'reputation traps'
- Redefine yourself when you have a new boss or start a new role

Managing your in-house reputation

Positioning

How and why do people get noticed at work? Is it always the most talented who rise – or the best self-publicists? A less cynical view is that individuals who achieve promotion instinctively align their personal reputations with the organization (or at least with the way senior decision-makers see the organization). They 'fit' and know how to communicate the fact.

Discovering how you are seen by others, and what gets said when your name comes up, is about understanding how well you match the organization you're in. You probably do this in detail when being interviewed for a role, but once you start the job your attention drifts. In a few years you may be surprised to discover that, like a piece of dusty luggage, you're no longer required on the voyage.

How hard should you work to impress? Whether you're extending your personal network or polishing your in-house image, the same question applies. Overexposure can easily mean that you're labelled as a shameless self-promoter. Underexposure means you may miss out on interesting opportunities or fail to build a sector reputation. Positioning is never just about your internal reputation. The wider market also gets to hear about you. This matters if you hope to be visible in the hidden job market (*see* Chapter 14).

Mentors increase perspective

You may worry too much or too little about how you are perceived. Many solve this by working with a mentor. The ideal mentor is someone more senior than you who can (a) decode the organization better than you, and (b) provide an objective picture of how well you fit. Even if the relationship is informal, this is someone who can tell you whether people wince or smile when your name comes up. Mentors will help you to understand promotion criteria (both the official process and the unwritten rules). They will provide big clues about how others see you – and what you can do about it.

'Many successful professionals will tell you that they got where they are with the help of support. Wise mentors are impartial, they make you reflect, challenge you, broaden your horizons and are a terrific sounding board.'

Ruth Winden, social media expert & career coach

Learn the difference between activity and contribution

Test your assumptions about how people ascend the promotion ladder. We often believe that colleagues get promoted because they put in strong performances year after year, reflected in positive appraisals. If you've worked hard but missed out on promotions, you feel baffled – what else do you need to do to get noticed?

Analysis of real promotion experiences suggests that people achieve advancement because they are noticed – but moments of visibility are often brief. Working hard all year round is often less impactful than being observed on one or two occasions by senior staff. People who make decisions about your future do so using very limited information. Your work reputation is built on soundbites. You're remembered for a succinct verbal report you delivered to a board meeting. You worked on a highly visible project. You shone on a secondment or when covering for a manager. You came up with a good solution. It could simply be that your name comes up regularly and your attitude is seen as positive.

Take an 'outside in' view of your role – looking at your job from the perspective of an impartial observer. Would an observer see and understand what you contribute? What would be missing if you were off work on observation day? What would an observer hear if your name is mentioned when you're out of the room?

'The truth is we all create images of others within work, e.g. risk taker, reliable, innovator, inflexible, influencer, deliverer. Career success comes from identifying what your image is and then looking to make it work within the prevailing context. Just as people talk about situational leadership where leaders need different styles for different situations, there are situational careers. Your career can flourish in one situation because there is a good match between you and the context and decline when that context changes.'

Carole Pemberton, Visiting Professor at
University of Ulster Business School and author of
Coaching to Solutions

Success at work depends on the decisions you take to manage your visibility and reputation. Learn how to reinforce the idea that you are focused on outcomes that really matter to the people who hired you. In other words: *working hard on the things that matter.*Volunteer for pilot schemes and multidisciplinary projects. Show how your work is aligned with the issues being discussed at the highest levels in your organization.

INCREASING YOUR VISIBILITY	
Events where you have little control or influence	**Events where you can exert control or influence**
You stand in for someone more senior who is on holiday.	You use the chance of covering an absence to show that you're a safe pair of hands prepared to make or postpone difficult decisions.
A senior manager sits in on a meeting where you are leading the discussion.	You treat the event as if it were an audition for the next role you hope to gain in the organization.
Key decision-makers are in the room when you make a presentation.	You prepare not just your content but how you present with equal attention, knowing that senior staff may make a snap decision about your future based on this moment of enhanced visibility.
Your boss witnesses you dealing with a difficult staff member.	You share with your boss what you learned from this difficult work conversation, and seek ideas for performing even better if handling a similar problem in future.

You learn new skills in your own time.	You negotiate new learning opportunities at work and then seek opportunities to solve work problems using your newly acquired skills.
You do something beyond the call of duty.	Record written customer feedback and pass it on when you have a review. Share with colleagues the strategies that got results.
You're praised in public and feel embarrassed.	Practise saying thank you when praised.
You perform tasks to an excellent standard, and develop some great short cuts.	Seek opportunities to share your expertise by training or coaching others.

The dangers of a solo performance

Workplace image is not achieved in isolation and is strongly connected to the reputation of your team, boss and organization. You can shine as an individual, but many people talk about the way that working in a great team was a career boost, or the way that a particular culture and leadership style brought out their talents.

One way of improving your reputation at work is to share information more frequently. Sharing rather than retaining information runs the risk that someone will run off with your ideas, but generally adds to positive team-working. Besides, sharing information can often be a subtle way of talking about what you've discovered, learned and achieved. If you have successes to talk about, focus on how learning from them can help the organization.

Hero or zero

Alastair Campbell, Tony Blair's director of communications and strategy, disclosed how media can shift a politician's reputation overnight – 'from hero to zero'. One day a political figure is idolized by the public and the party heirarchy, but a single day of bad news can turn this individual into a liability or has-been.

Jean-François Manzoni and Jean-Louis Barsoux are authors of *The Set-Up-To-Fail Syndrome* (Harvard Business Press, 2002), which provides insights into what can happen when you start a new role. Managers form a strong impression about a new employee very quickly, after seeing them in action just once or twice. Manzoni and Barsoux show that managers decide instinctively at this point if you're a star performer or not worth investing in. Unconsciously, interesting and challenging work is given to those perceived as 'stars'. On an equally unconscious level others are 'set up to fail' – given work where they are less likely to perform well. The situation is worsened by ineffective feedback and poorer support for people considered not to have a brilliant future.

Your boss's initial judgement about whether you're a winner or loser is instinctive and based on the first few times you're noticed. When starting a new role or when your boss changes (*see below*) make sure you broadcast quiet competence and audible enthusiasm.

Reading your boss's style

The way you are seen in the workplace is often a direct reflection of the quality of the relationship you have with your line manager. You can be set up to fail, or your manager could become your champion and advocate.

Learn to use contact time effectively. Frequently popping in for a 'quick word' distracts and reinforces the idea that you have problems working unsupervised. Plan discussions with care, using an informal verbal agenda ('I'd like to talk to you about three things — have you got a couple of minutes?'). Keep your boss informed (but not over-informed). Communicate concisely in a weekly report. Use a 20/5 approach — a 1-page document that takes you 20 minutes to write, and your boss 5 minutes to read.

Work out your boss's thinking style. Is your boss focused on detail, or the big picture? Is your boss naturally democratic, consultative or autocratic? Learn how your boss prefers to receive new information and questions. Don't double-check every detail; learn where you can act on your own initiative and where you need to seek authorization. As you gain experience you may find that 'seeking forgiveness' after a decision offers more freedom of action than always seeking prior approval — but that means you have to know your superior well.

Try not to hand back problems delegated to you, because that can be read in a number of negative ways. Say you'll analyse the task and get back within 24 hours if any predictable snags come to light. If your working style irritates your boss (perhaps you believe that a tidy desk is a sign of a sick mind), get over yourself and do things differently.

Asking for more

Statistically women earn less than men, and surveys show they feel less confident asking for a promotion or pay rise. The world of work feels unfair — abrasive, pushy men get top jobs, but the same quality in women is seen as aggressive and manipulative. Do you find it difficult to ask for what you want in the workplace? Are you patiently waiting to be noticed? This behaviour can signal not just a lack of ambition but lack of commitment. It may arise from modesty (*see* Chapter 5), but can easily signal a lack of interest in career progression. Busy managers can see ambition in black-and-white terms: you're either full-on ambitious or you're meek and mild. Look around for mid-range role models – people who ask quietly but firmly.

It usually costs an employer more to replace you than to renegotiate your career deal, but don't wander into reviews unprepared. If you want a pay rise, offer a work-related reason. Talk about what you have added to your role – with tangible examples of where you have saved money, delighted customers, won business or deputized for someone more senior. Practise by negotiating deals and discounts in your life outside work – it sharpens up your playful resistance to the word 'no'.

Make a business case rather than an emotional one – anything that sounds like 'I feel undervalued' is giving your manager a tricky problem. If your boss hates surprises, send a written summary before you meet. Have a Plan B ready in case of refusal – ask for an early review, or for something your employer can provide with little pain (e.g. a learning opportunity, attachment to an interesting project, or new tasks).

Learn how self-projection is seen in your work culture. One senior banking professional told me his rule for direct reports: 'no campaigning for promotion'. If what you're doing sounds like a pitch for promotion, he doesn't want to know. On the other hand, he and his colleagues agreed that people seem to think that just working hard will get them advancement. If senior managers don't know you're interested in promotion (or personal development, or being stretched by a new challenge), they won't offer it. There are dangers of being too 'me first', but also dangers in keeping your head down and not saying anything.

Some push negotiations until the shouting starts, but if you're not a natural table-thumper, don't wait for opportunity to find you – the world of work is too busy to notice understated performances. *See* the checklist below.

Asking for better terms without resorting to banging the table

1 **Be clear of your 'offer'.** Know what you are good at, the skills you use best and put together a list of what you have learned and achieved at work over the past 12 months. Find an authentic way of communicating three or four key items of information.

2 **Decode how you're seen before you try to change the picture.** Managing the perception of others is vital to getting promoted. Get feedback on how you appear to others and how you can change their view. A mentor will help.

3 **Ensure you're visible to decision-makers.** Make the most of opportunities when you will be seen by senior staff (particularly during presentations). Performance at high-visibility moments can be career altering.

4 **Think about what your employer needs.** Work hard, but keep a focus on the things that really matter to your organization and your boss. What are the key areas for business performance? How can you spot 'quick wins' that help you and your employer?

5 **Look and sound the part.** Invest in clothes that make you look as though you've already been promoted, and behave the same way. Sound positive without saying 'yes' to everything, and avoid getting drawn into cynical conversations.

6 **Learn authentic negotiation.** Don't bang the table or complain, but ask firmly and politely for a new working deal that reflects where you have added value. Be prepared to ask more than once.

Reputation traps

Career blocks can arise from external circumstances, difficult colleagues or confused goals, but we're also capable of sabotaging our own careers and falling into traps.

You might feel trapped by an inaccurate reputation – you've become known as the go-to person on IT solutions, but that's not how you see your future. Offer a gentle challenge to assumptions: 'I expect you think I'm mainly interested in research. Actually, I've really enjoyed some of the training I've delivered recently…'

You might find yourself working in an area of a business that seems irrelevant. Reputations can also be tarnished by working on projects or products that have failed. You might be associated with a leader who has fallen from grace, with out-of-date technology, or a former employer that has been disgraced. A mentor should be able to tell you how things stand, warts and all, and then help you rebuild.

If you get stuck in a dead-end role and feel your career is on hold, be aware of your perceived attitude, especially if you sound jaded or cynical. Your water-cooler reputation can change from 'on message and useful' to 'resistant to change' faster than you think. Staff are seen as assets not just because of skills, but for less tangible factors such as sounding positive and open to change.

Take particular care if someone is flattering you into taking a role that is a perceived career trap. You don't want to disappoint the person recommending you, and you might think it's dangerous to turn down a promotion. However, be clear if a role will enhance your CV. If required, find a constructive way of turning down the offer. Don't just say 'no': use the opportunity to talk about how you can add value: 'If you really want to get value out of me, give me a chance to...' Be most cautious if you're offered a poisoned chalice role, with conflicting objectives and poor resources, where no one lasts more than 12 months.

Sticking doggedly to your job profile is the biggest career trap of all. Think of your job description as a starting point rather than a destination. Interrogate your job for possibilities of growth. Research your own employer and its changing needs. Look at the way your organization uses outside consultants. What could you do to fill the same need?

You can also fall into a reputation trap by being seen as a poor manager. This could easily be a matter of perception rather than reality. Your superiors probably won't have first-hand experience of your style as a manager – but they will judge you by the results of your team, and by problems with personnel retention or regular complaints. The performance of your subordinates – and maintaining team relationships – reflects on you.

Handling organizational politics

What do we mean by organizational politics? Some feel all competition is healthy, others enjoy 'getting their retaliation in first'. Some enjoy points scoring, winning and losing. Others find it a confusing game of deception, manoeuvring and sometimes even sabotage. Internal politics can easily result in ingrained cynicism, pulling in different directions, and demotivation. The result can be destructive – customers are lost and talent moves on.

In a 'political' culture the temptation is to side with the strongest faction or play by house rules. Soon you're conniving with 'silo' behaviour, sitting on information rather than passing it on, allowing others to fail. Attend to potential minefields. If you're initiating a project, think about who will feel threatened. Whose pet project will you trash? Who will feel aggrieved if you claim an idea as your own, or irritated by your suggestions for reorganization? Find out from colleagues which past initiatives have made waves.

If someone is deliberately undermining your reputation, that's when you need to act with caution; for example, if you're being trashed to recruitment agencies by former colleagues, or blamed by your boss for a mistake that was not yours. Perhaps a former boss you didn't get on with is putting new employers off. If you need to repair the way you're seen, you need the objective help of a coach or mentor. How big is the problem? Do you try to influence the situation, or is it wiser to keep silent?

Hitting 'restart' with a new boss or role

There are key moments when you can really take control of your workplace image. One is where you have a new boss, who may have heard something about you, but first impressions carry more weight. Sharpen up your image – buy smarter work clothes. Contribute ideas, solutions and short-cuts. Think of your first two weeks with a new boss as an important audition. Offer solutions, helpful information – anything that creates the picture that you're a great asset.

Your first three months in a job also have a huge impact on the way you're seen. Try not to criticize the way the job is already done; introduce new ideas with great caution. Make tentative suggestions by sharing methods you have used and introducing pilot schemes rather than telling people how things should be done. Challenging everything from day one means you'll probably be trashing someone else's work. Don't make too many promises at this stage because you probably have no idea how many you can deliver.

Learn operating procedures quickly so you understand the rhythms of the job and pick up culture and language. Conformity may be boring, but it keeps you out of trouble in your first few weeks. It also signals your ability to learn systems quickly. Make a special effort to find information brokers – the people who know who does what, and who to ask. Aim to implement two or three changes that are low on cost and high on imagination. Make sure you follow up – or your reputation will be 'talks the talk, but...'

Top 10 tips for protecting your reputation

1 Be aware of political minefields. Distance yourself from 'toxic' attitudes and people.

2 Work alongside others who have better political 'radar' than you.

3 Watch your back. Are you treading on someone else's toes? Check how far your success means someone else's failure.

4 Keep integrity as your surprise card. Be clear about what you are not prepared to do to win. Be honest, be consistent.

5 Praise regularly, criticize cautiously. Remember your mother's advice: 'If you can't say anything nice, don't say anything at all.' Avoid gossip. It's fun, but watch where discreet observation becomes character assassination.

6 Look for WIN/WIN. Even in a highly politicized environment, it's possible to offer solutions that help you and your employer.

7 Be consistent. It's no use having integrity one day and being a conniving manipulator the next.

8 Do what you say you will do. Fail to deliver (without good reason) and everything you say becomes an empty promise.

9 Lose gracefully. If others jump the queue, push you aside or outmanoeuvre you, don't be tempted to play by the same rules. He who lives by the sword…

10 If organizational politics threaten your integrity too often, it may be time to move out. When you do so, talk about what attracts you to your new role, not what's pushing you out of the old one.

14
Projecting into the job market

This chapter helps you to:

- Apply what you have learned to a career move
- Understand how softer forms of self-projection build relationships and strong networks when you're exploring new roles
- Navigate the hidden job market
- Plant messages out there about what you're seeking and what you have to offer

Looking for a job means working with other people

Stepping away from the passive herd

Measured self-projection, effective relationships and taking control of your reputation – these matter hugely when you're trying to get into a new job. This chapter applies this thinking to career change. For more ideas, see one of my career books, particularly *How To Get A Job You Love*.

When you're job-seeking it feels harder than ever to project yourself confidently. It can easily feel like you're begging for an interview. Wanting to avoid the discomfort of networking, career changers choose more passive behaviours. They keep their distance by email rather than picking up the phone. They fire off half-hearted applications for jobs they don't fully understand. Advertised jobs are 'candidate magnets' attracting hundreds of applications. If you don't very clearly match the selection criteria, you'll fall at the first hurdle. More passively still, they put their trust in online applications, even though the hit rate is low – for most people the end result is cold silence. Yet online searching feels productive, looks like work and seems a great alternative to unsavoury networking.

Relationships, not screens, shorten job search time

Staring at screens and keeping the world at a distance has consequences for self-projection. It means you rely on your CV or online profile to shape what people know about you. Everything depends on your writing skills (*see* Chapter 11), and by avoiding human contact you severely reduce the chance that you will be remembered.

When I help someone find a new role, I ask one question at the end of their programme: 'What would you do differently next time?' Nearly every time the answer is 'I would start talking to people earlier'. This isn't a nice add-on, or a strategy adopted only by movers and shakers – it's the best way of shortening a job search.

You've heard the line *It's not what you know, it's who you know*. It's a convenient phrase to hide behind. Yes, some jobs are given out by family, friends, schoolmates or others who share some tribal allegiance. Let's rephrase the sentence: *It's not who you know, it's who you CHOOSE TO GET TO KNOW*. You can get a job through several channels, but the most likely route is through somebody you talk to in the next three months. Whatever your age, class or background, jobs go to people who are visible.

Multi-strategy job search means working smarter, not harder. Combine predictable steps (chasing vacancies and registering with agencies) with more active tactics (such as talking to people in interesting roles and sectors). Make direct approaches to organizations not currently advertising, build relationships with recruitment agencies and research like mad. Don't kid yourself that spending all day in front of a computer screen is the best use of your time. Use the Internet outside normal working hours – during the day get in front of people even if they're just friends. At least once a week dress smartly and meet someone who can move you forward. You will get practice in talking about yourself, pick up ideas, but you'll also feel much more 'real' – and employable – than sitting at home in your slippers.

Initial impact when you go to the job market

What you say to people about yourself when you start job hunting may form your long-term market reputation. If you start out communicating frustration or disappointment, that's what people remember. Bad news travels easily. Good news travels when you fire it up and set it on its way. Your good

WHAT TO TELL PEOPLE ABOUT YOUR JOB SEARCH	
Tell them	**Don't tell them**
Your career ideas	Why you're unhappy to be on the job market
Questions you have in need of answers	You're sick of applying for jobs or talking to recruitment agencies
What specific roles you're looking for	You're waiting for other people to make things happen for you
What you've discovered so far	
What you've already enjoyed about exploratory conversations	
Work sectors you find fascinating	You don't know what you're looking for
Organizations you want to be closer to	You think your CV isn't working
People you're trying to reach	

news doesn't need to be hyped-up – simply mentioning what you're interested in is enough to convey enthusiasm and begin to open doors. The way you look for a job is taken as a strong indication of how you will perform in a job. If you're diffident, sound like you're begging, or if you're pushy, employers assume this is how you act in a new role.

Chapter 11 looked at maximizing attention while minimizing irritation when you send something in writing. The same applies to the way you interact with contacts when you're job-seeking. Busy people dislike having their time wasted by answering obvious questions. They prefer to be informed, rather than sold to, and mistrust candidates who make unlikely or naive claims. They want to meet people focused on organizational needs (*see* Connection Statements below). Employers respond well to applicants who can describe their strengths without over-egging or false modesty – and individuals whose online presence backs up their claims.

The hidden job market

We know that some jobs are never advertised and sometimes only one candidate is interviewed for a job. People are tipped off that a job is coming up, or an organization creates jobs around them. Risk avoidance means employers are attracted by people who are already on their radar. This could be the office temp or intern, or it could be someone they've met only recently. That's the hidden job market. As employers discover cheap and painless ways of falling across good candidates without advertising, job seekers increasingly have to dip their toes in the shark-infested waters of networking and making direct approaches to organizations who aren't issuing vacancies.

Projecting yourself into the hidden job market is about making sure your name is mentioned for the right reason – when someone mentions a problem or an opportunity, your skill set is mentioned as a good fit. As Chapter 4 outlined, if you've planted the right messages, the right information is passed on. This information shouldn't surprise you – you've put it there. It should be a close match to the typical needs of organizations on your target list.

Ignoring the hidden job market will mean you extend your job search time and miss some of the most interesting opportunities on the planet. They won't be in the Help Wanted section, because right now they're brewing away in the brain of someone you might just meet, pretty soon, if you simply start asking the best career question ever: 'Who else should I be talking to?'

Planting messages matters more when you want a change of career

You may be thinking about a complete career change; perhaps you've always worked in banking but now you want to move into property development. If you want to make a sector change, the critical step is always to talk to people about their experience. Seek conversations with people who have made the leap ahead of you. How did they make the changes they achieved? What did they do right? What mistakes did they make? If the obvious route to a new role is closed, what back door routes are available?

Think about what happens if you apply for a job without having these conversations. Lacking sector knowledge and obvious work experience, you'll struggle to get onto a shortlist. You may have transferable skills, but you haven't learned to make them sound credible. In other words, you're shooting blind. Spend more time than you think you need having exploratory conversations. One great spin-off is that you start to pick up insider language which, used carefully, shows that your interest in a new sector is more than a pipe dream.

It's no use trying to woo employers if you have no idea what presses their buttons. Do your homework – if you don't it's difficult to convince an employer that you're interested. If you get a meeting, spend at least two hours thoroughly researching the organization on the Internet. Additionally, speak to people who know what the organization is trying to achieve, and the kind of people they are currently hiring. Look at organization websites, articles and discussion groups so you can speak knowledgeably about the industry.

Yes, but what do I say about myself?

Question the assumption that your primary activity in a job search is selling yourself. There will come a point when you need to clearly set out your stall, as discussed below, but don't fall into the trap of believing that the best focus of any conversation is you.

Let's imagine you're attending a trade event and exhibition because you know that several interesting employers will be represented. You could do what average job hunters do and walk round in silence collecting leaflets. However, you want to be remembered as someone with potentially useful experience. Also you want to be introduced to people back at head office. So you turn up, and every instinct says 'communicate, communicate'. Think again. Your most powerful pieces of equipment are stuck on each side of your head. Listen, absorb, keep discovering. Go to the event armed with some good research, but also have plenty of good questions ready. Occasionally, when it matters, have a quick summary of what you're offering.

Look at this from the perspective of people staffing exhibition stands at this event. Foregrounding the fact that you're a job hunter may seem relevant to you, but it's of little interest to your listener. If your first words are 'I'm looking for a job' they worry that you will ask for a referral to Human Resources, or you will ask about suitable vacancies likely to crop up. They're also hoping to avoid looking at your CV.

Say something briefly about your interest, but focus on asking brilliant questions based on your homework. Throw in snippets of information from previous discoveries – this shows that you really are interested in conversations about organizations, sectors and trends, not looking for a covert job interview. It also confirms that you're serious about career change not just imagining possible futures.

Stay hungry for information

Avoid the mistake of thinking a good job search conversation is a chance to showcase your abilities. The best ones begin relationships, but they're mainly about discovery. Put information gathering at the heart of your questions. For example, 'I'm really interested in what's going on in event management at the moment. Tell me – what sorts of venues do you find are the biggest headaches?' ... I've read that these mega-venues are a technical nightmare – is that right? Fascinating... You know, I was talking to the technical team at GMEX recently and they told me... Have you experienced that? ... And how much of that is outsourced these days? Really... who else is doing work like that?'

Notice anything about this conversation? It's nearly all about the person you're talking to. It works because people generally find it easy to talk about their work, as long as your questions are interesting and don't go on forever. You're focusing on a world they know well, so these questions are easy to answer. You're showing that you've done some genuine research which suggests that this is really interesting to you, not just small talk. Ensure your language conveys genuine enthusiasm ('what fascinates me...')

Now the only question to tag on to a great discussion is one aimed at unearthing new contacts: 'This has been amazingly helpful, thank you. Who else do you think I should be talking to if I'm going to get the big picture?' – or something along those lines. However, you probably can't get there without some explanation about why you're interested and what you're hoping to do with the answers. This means setting out your stall. Many would see this as the perfect moment for an elevator pitch, but that might feel risky as well as uncomfortable – as if all your questions have been simply an excuse to get a chance to deliver your 'buy me' speech.

What's the point of just gathering information when I want to be noticed?

You're asking questions, but you're getting far more than information in return. You're projecting yourself softly, subtly, as the kind of person who might make a credible addition to a short-list. You're becoming someone whose name might just come up when a decision-maker in an organization is thinking about filling a role.

Benefits of information-gathering questions

1 You start to acquire genuine sector knowledge, which is critically helpful if you are sector-hopping.
2 You pick up further insider language, at a deeper level.
3 You will hear people talking about industry stars – top performers – giving you big clues about the skills that are most highly sought in your target sector.
4 In a job search you pick up useful information about organizations which are growing or have other talent needs.
5 You build a network, zone by zone (*see* Chapter 10). Some people you meet in this way will still be sharing information with you five years from now.

---

6 People remember you for your enthusiasm, commitment to finding things out, and for your short Connection Statement. Remembering you can be enough to generate an introduction, a referral and sometimes even a recommendation.

7 Because you're a genuine enquirer, not asking for help in an embarrassing or hard sell way, you should get a good answer to the question 'Who should I be talking to next?'

Connection Statements

Try a **Connection Statement** instead. That's a shorter, more natural response at this point in the conversation. You're really saying 'Here's why this conversation is useful to me...' rather than 'Phew – now we've got that over I can talk about myself'. A Connection Statement doesn't work hard at selling, but is a helpful explanation – your X links to my Y. It should only take a couple of breaths to say, for example:

'Thank you – what you're telling me is really interesting – it's a sector I'm getting really fascinated by. What I've learned from a number of conversations is that my background in project management could be useful. Does that make sense to you?'

You've got across a short statement about your sector experience, knowledge and skills, but you've threaded it into a conversation neatly by expressing gratitude for what you've learned and explaining how your background offers valid connections.

However, sometimes you will receive an explicit invitation to set out your stall – 'Tell me about yourself – what's your background?' or a simple 'What about you?'. If you haven't said much about yourself, ask some questions and use a Connection Statement. Or link past to present – talk briefly about your experience but bring the conversation back to the here and now: '... which is why I am trying to speak to as many cutting-edge organizations as I can...'

Planting messages

Remember how you planted messages in Chapter 4 – remembering the power of three? The same thing applies here. When recommending potential candidates, or simply passing on people who are interested, we normally say only two or three things by explanation.

If there are only three information 'slots' available when someone mentions your name, wouldn't it be a shame if those slots were used up with negative information: 'You might consider Mark ... of course, he's feeling rather beaten up about redundancy. He wishes he had jumped ship earlier. He isn't getting a good reaction from the agencies he's approached.' Here's someone who has clearly not had enough Zone 1 conversations (*see* Chapter 10) – he's going to important contacts but projecting anxiety not employability.

Make sure that you show excitement and a hunger to find out more. Enthusiasm is remembered and opens doors. If you've done the right homework you'll come across as a serious and committed enquirer and you'll be passed along. You don't need a series of 'I am brilliant at...' statements – even if you felt comfortable making them, they're more likely to convey egotism than energy. Use Connection Statements as outlined above, just saying a couple of things about why your experience is useful to future employers.

Take another look at your CV and online profile

Spend more time thinking about how people will interpret your CV and LinkedIn page (*see* Chapter 11). Don't be under the illusion that you should send out your CV widely in the early stages of your job search. It's far better to talk to people about your career ideas and to gather information than to send out a poorly drafted document that closes more doors than it opens.

In conversation the first few seconds conveys an immediate impression. The same is true of the first 50 words of your CV. Do you get the most important facts (role specialism, background, sector experience, skill set) across quickly? Remembering Chapter 11, does clarity trump persuasion? In other words, are you trying to sell yourself by using what you think is influential language but ends up as cliché – *A highly motivated team player with exceptional leadership skills…*

Lazy communicators simply lift phrases from example CVs found on the Internet, but that's no way to differentiate yourself. Too often when people hope to stand out they achieve the opposite, using the same tired old language as everyone else. Trying to sell your personality on paper is largely a waste of time. Bullet point skills and achievements, beginning each line with a strong verb (*Created…Initiated…Organized…Led…*). Some job advertisements contain examples of energized language you can adapt to fit your evidence, and as you get better at matching it to employer needs, you'll get more interviews.

Use the same care when describing yourself on your LinkedIn profile. Look at a range of profiles. If you can't detect overselling ask someone who can – people with hiring experience are usually good at showing what makes a candidate attractive online. Avoid explicitly flagging up issues that might worry a reader, such as hints that your career is in difficulty. On LinkedIn there's a big difference between talking about the kinds of projects you'd love to be approached about and saying that you are 'available for exciting projects' – overemphasizing the fact that your diary is full of gaps. You'll see many profiles stating 'seeking new opportunities' on LinkedIn, and most sound like weak requests for affirmation. You'll get better results including information about skills, projects undertaken, the names of organizations worked for, specialisms and other key words likely to be picked up by recruiters. Employers want to know about your skills, not the fact that you're out of work.

Be as clear in your online profile as you need to be when you're explaining yourself to a stranger. Zena Everett draws on extensive recruitment experience when she argues that candidates:

'...are too generic about their skills and vague about their career objectives. They say "I can do anything in marketing" rather than "I really understand the 40-something woman and her retail buying patterns so am particularly interested in a role that enables me to use this expertise". You'll be hired because you can solve particular problems rather than just because you are a good all-rounder. Think back when you were involved in a hiring decision. Did you say "let's get a nice person into the team who has good office skills" or was it more specific "let's get someone in who is really good on the phone and will manage the team's diary for us"?'

Zena Everett, careers coach

Top 10 messages from this chapter

1 Become a standout candidate by actively building relationships rather than passively hiding behind computer screens.
2 Start talking to people early in your job search.
3 Make research a bigger priority than simply sending out job applications.
4 Don't set out to tell people why you should be hired; set out to find out more about organizations and sectors.

5 Ensure your approaches are backed up by in-depth research to help you spot trends and pick up insider language.

6 Pitch some great, well-researched questions before attempting to talk about your career aims.

7 Relationship-building and planting positive messages about your enthusiasm and experience are key to cracking the hidden job market.

8 If you want to do something a little different, you're going to have to reach out earlier and more extensively.

9 Learn Connection Statements to make a link between your enquiries and what you have to offer.

10 Obtain objective advice to make sure that your CV and online profile offer clarity and hit the right tone.

15

Start the easy way and get results

This chapter helps you to:

- Adopt strategies you can use TOMORROW
- Work right up to the edge of your comfort zone
- Be more effective in your next warm-up conversation
- Use sample scripts to kick-start activity

Do what works for you rather than trying to do everything

By now you'll have got the idea that you are not trying to flip your personality from one state to another, to magically transform yourself into a seasoned communicator or networker. What you're doing is increasing your influence by working with what you've got, building on what feels authentic.

If you're a quieter person, don't try to work across the grain. Do things in the way that feels least alien. Go to an event early – chatting to the host is an easy way to get introduced to the first people who arrive. Offer to help – it's much easier to chat to people if you're in role, even if that's just pouring coffee or giving out badges. If you feel drained by conversation, don't beat yourself up about it. Decide how much of an event you need to attend in order to hear and say the right things; decide how much you can do without feeling exhausted (Susan Cain, author of *Quiet*, suggests you adopt a 'quota' of meetings and events – attending a set number each month even if you feel

you'd rather stay at home). If you're more comfortable standing quietly on the edge of things picking up the vibe, do that
for a while and then decide how to use the limited amount of
energy available to you by having two or three conversations.
Avoid at all costs sounding desperate or out of your depth – key
discussion topics for Zone 2 (*see* Chapter 10).

If there is a particular person you want to talk to, do your
best to make that conversation happen (*see* Chapter 6 for subtler approaches which leave the door open for a future conversation). Remember that you don't have to talk to everyone at
an event. If you feel that you've done what your energy allows,
move on. You may miss something, but often the most important conversations happen relatively quickly when introductions are made, and you don't need to stay to the bitter end.
After all, it's better to do things within your working limits
than to do nothing at all. However, do find another event soon.
Even making one warm connection makes a two-hour event
far more productive than spending a whole week staring at a
screen.

Watch out for three well-known avoidance strategies. The
first is not turning up at all. The next is going to events but
remaining in silent observer mode, feeling you have nothing
important to say. Try putting your focus on making other people feel comfortable; ask them how they're enjoying the event
and what interests them. The third avoidance strategy is attach-
ing yourself to one person as a conversational safety net and
speaking just to that one person all evening.

If you know there are people to reach out to but can't find
the courage or stamina to do so, try turning it into a game.
Reward yourself for every step that takes you closer. When you
manage to reach someone on the phone, give yourself a nice
lunch. Once a face-to-face meeting is in the diary, treat yourself
to something smart to wear. Turning the process into a game is
a great way of reframing.

'As If' reframing

Chapter 1 looked at how we're comfortable promoting a product or service but hate talking about ourselves. This book has shown a number of ways to get past this mental block, including the technique of talking about what fascinates you rather than describing yourself. Reframing is another strategy: rather than tackling the problem head-on, come at it from another angle.

Acting 'As If', championed by psychologist Richard Wiseman, is not just about thinking differently, but doing things differently. One example would be that it's much easier to pick up the phone to tell people about a great offer than to talk about your skills. So, act as if you are in fact talking about a book or a webpage – a history of events that you can hold at a distance rather than your biography. You might also try acting as if you are talking about someone else. This isn't the same as pretending to be someone different – nor does it mean saying 'she' or 'he' rather than 'I'. It means starting in a more neutral mode like 'the strategy that most interests me is...' and taking emphasis off the word 'me', and putting it on to more neutral words. So: 'the *strategy* that most *interests* me is...' – the listener's tuned in to those keywords, not 'me'. Contrast this with 'What *I* enjoy most' or 'For *me*, the main thing is...'

Reframing and then acting 'as if' can also apply very successfully to how you reach out to people. Think about how much easier it is to make connections for a colleague than for yourself. At a social event it's much easier to be the one making introductions than the one hoping to be introduced (a good reason to go early so you can act as facilitator). Acting as if you are doing it for someone else means that you tend to be more professional, anticipating that someone will say yes rather than always anticipating 'no'.

Celebrate knock-backs

When you're reaching out to people, you will experience silence – someone doesn't return your call, for example. Someone promises to make a connection but fails to do so. Don't take these natural outcomes personally. People are busy and you are not the most important thing on their agendas. Even the most accomplished salespeople know they will hear 'no' three or four times more often than 'yes'. Don't forget that when you are relatively uncommitted, a fortnight can feel like a long time to wait for someone to return a call. To a busy executive in the middle of another round of restructuring this time goes past in a blink. Collect and celebrate non-responses as blanks you will fill in at some future date.

Cultivate resilience by designing a personal scorecard (*see* Chapter 8), rewarding yourself as you get closer to the people you want to speak to. Don't rush so fast that you stumble when you reach them, but don't delay so long that you never have the conversations that matter.

Practice

In his book *Outliers* Malcolm Gladwell shows what it takes to become a concert standard musician or an outstanding computer programmer. Mastery in any field, Gladwell argues, takes about 10,000 hours of practice.

The seriously good news about self-projection is that you don't need to be world class. You just need to improve, one step at a time. So rather than setting the bar out of reach, do one new thing differently every day. Everyone gets better at networking and communication with practice. Yes, everyone, even the people who have to be dragged kicking and screaming to the task. The fascinating thing is that these people will eventually tell their friends that learning to reach out to people provided their biggest breakthroughs.

Use the zone system outlined in Chapter 10. Start with people you find easy to talk to. Practise, learn, adjust. If you're at a networking event or conference, chat to people who aren't top of your 'must-meet' list first; warm up before you approach the key people you really want to meet.

Don't worry about preparing a killer speech or elevator pitch. It's usually better to find out more about the person you are talking to. Use this book to learn how to ask questions that keep conversations alive. Rehearse connection statements and a quick summary of your work experience.

Starter Scripts

To enable you to move forward quickly, there are some outline scripts to be found in the Appendix. You may hate the idea of using scripted material. How can you feel authentic using these words rather than your own? Don't panic. The scripts are meant as starting points to enable you to come up with words that work for you. Each script is cross-referenced with the relevant part of the Zone System (*see* Chapter 10):

Starter Script	Zone
A – Testing Your Material	Zone 2
B – Information Gathering	Zone 3
C – Networking Appointments	Zones 4 & 5
D – Networking Encounters	Zone 6

Please note that each of the four scripts set out in the Appendix misses out one vital element – small talk. It's so local and personal it can't be pre-scripted. You could be talking about location, weather, office decor or mutual friends. Just don't miss out that vital first step in any conversation – start easy and comfortable.

10 myth-busting tips about communicating your abilities to others

1 You don't have to be an extrovert to communicate well. Introverts often say things more thoughtfully and make better listeners.

2 You don't have to have a great contacts list. If you ask intelligent questions, don't waste people's time and don't oversell yourself people are generally very happy to pass your name on.

3 You don't have to ring people cold. Starting a conversation 'you don't know me but' is a real conversation killer. Ask people to make introductions, not just give you names.

4 You don't have to sell yourself. In fact, anything that looks and sounds like overt self-promotion puts people off.

5 You don't have to have one goal in mind. Tell people about the range of things that interest you.

6 It's not all about you. Good conversations where you impress people involve active listening.

7 You don't have to start brilliantly. Everyone gets better at networking with practice; start with people who are easy to approach.

8 You don't need a killer speech or elevator pitch, but do work on summary material and Connection Statements.

9 You don't have to boast. This makes you a boring and not very credible conversationalist. Talk about the things that energize you.

10 You won't run out of contacts – not if you keep asking the question 'Who else should I be talking to...?

Appendix

Starter Script	Zone
A –Testing Your Material	Zone 2
B – Information Gathering	Zone 3
C – Networking Appointments	Zones 4 & 5
D – Networking Encounters	Zone 6

STARTER SCRIPT A – Testing Your Material

(Use this script to prepare for Zone 2 conversations)

Introduction

- As I mentioned, I'd like to get better at talking about what I do before getting in front of other people. Can I practise on you? Can you give me some feedback about what I could do better?
- You're much better at talking to people than I am. Can I run something by you?
- This might come out wrong, but here goes...

The kind of help I need

- Can you help me summarize my main skills?
- If I talk about my recent work projects can you help me identify some good evidence?
- Can you help me think about my strengths?
- What do you think are the main things that I should say if somebody asks me to describe myself?

- Can we discuss my CV or my LinkedIn profile? What do these say to you?

Feedback

- What do I need to think about before speaking to people I don't know so well?
- What kind of people should I be aiming to reach?
- What am I getting wrong? What am I getting right?
- What should I work on?

Next steps

- Thanks – that's great. Can I have a think about your feedback today and then come back to you?
- Brilliant. Can I see you in a few days' time and try something different, and this time ask you some questions?

STARTER SCRIPT B – Information Gathering

(Use this script to prepare for Zone 3 conversations)

Introduction

- As I mentioned, I'm here to practise reaching out to people. This might come out wrong, but here goes...

Questions about the person you're talking to

- Can I start by asking you about the work you do? How did you get into it?
- What's changing in your sector?
- Which other organizations are important players?
- Who are the established businesses? Who's new?
- Which organizations and people should I be looking up?
- What websites or publications should I follow to find out more?
- Who should I be talking to next?

Feedback

- That's great, really helpful.
- Normally at this stage people say 'tell me a little bit about you'. Would you ask me that? Would you ask as if you don't know me and give me some feedback on my answer?

Next steps

- Thanks very much. Can we go back to the contacts you mentioned? Would any of them be happy to have the kind of conversation we've had today?

- Great. I hate ringing people cold – would you do me a big favour and phone ahead to tell them why I'd like a conversation? (Note: as Zone 2 in Chapter 10 explains, you might want to hold off on the 'next steps' phase outlined above. You might ask someone to hold fire on making introductions until you're a little more proficient).

STARTER SCRIPT C – Networking Appointments

(Use this script to prepare for Zone 4 and Zone 5 conversations)

Introduction

- Thanks for seeing me today. As I mentioned on the phone, I'm trying to talk to a range of people who really know this sector.

Questions about the person you're talking to

- What do you enjoy about your current line of work?
- What's the most exciting thing about your job? What's less interesting?
- How did you begin working in this sector? What attracted you to it?
- What changes have you seen in the past year or two?
- How has your job changed since you started here?
- What do you enjoy most about your role? What's your biggest headache?
- What other organizations should I be looking at?
- Where do people in this sector meet up?
- I'd really value your advice. Who should I speak to next?

STARTER SCRIPT D – Networking Encounters

(Use this script to prepare for Zone 6 conversations, and see also *Chapter 6 for more tips on drawing people into conversations)*

Breaking the ice at a conference or event

- You seem to be enjoying this. What's been the best bit for you?
- I'm finding this really stimulating. What about you?
- I wish I'd found this material/book/idea/speaker years ago. How long have you been a fan?
- What prompted you to put this event in your diary?
- I'm just thinking about how we might be able to put this stuff into practice. How do you think it might help you?

Questions about the person you're talking to

- Tell me about you – what do you enjoy most about the work you do?
- You know, I'm always interested in how people choose their careers. How did you get into your line of work?
- I know that sector has changed hugely. What changes have you seen?
- So you started at X. You must know Kate...? (cross-reference with people you've already met)
- How nice to meet someone else who studied history. How have you kept your interest going?

When they ask about you

- I'm here because I thought it would help me with the next project I'm leading.
- I've always been interested in this kind of thinking, ever since I started working in retail...
- I'm always looking for new ideas to put on the HR website I've been managing for the past five years. Are there other conferences you'd recommend?
- My background is in property sales, but I've had some great conversations recently with people working in industrial heritage. Does your work touch on that area at all? (*See* Chapter 14 on Connection Statements)

Next steps

- It's great to meet someone who really knows about the sector. Can I ask you for your card? If it's OK I'd love to ask you a couple of questions by email later this week.
- You mentioned one of your colleagues who's here tonight. Would you mind introducing me?
- It's really noisy here. Could I give you a quick call later in the week to round off our conversation?
- You clearly know your stuff. Who else do you think I should be talking to? Brilliant – is she here this evening?

Index